To Anthony and Nonno:
The alpha and omega of lifelong learning

Contents

Acknowledgments

First, I would like to thank the editors of Rowman and Littlefield, in particular Tom Koerner, for seeing the merit in my work and agreeing to its publication. I cannot thank enough the four colleagues who consented to contribute their thoughts and words to Chapter Six: Stephanie Aldrich, Gary Blomgren, Belle Coles, and Sue Dana. Numerous individuals read and commented upon the manuscript, providing me with useful insights and criticism—thank you Joan Burkhard, Loren Clews, Dr. Rosetta Cohen, Dr. Susan Dreyer Leon, Dr. Sam Intrator, Beth Keplinger, Robert Kramsky, KD Maynard, Casey Murrow, Sandy Pentak, Dr. Carol Rodgers, and Tara Toolan. As ever, I appreciate the love and support of my beautiful children: son Benjamin, daughter-in-law Pam, and grandson Anthony. They give me inspiration. Finally, I would probably get nothing done without the love of my life, my greatest supporter, and my personal bodhisattva: Nina.

Introduction

At first glance, school curriculum may appear to be a simple concept. Teach the kids how to read and write, perform mathematics and science, and know some history. Basically, help the students to learn the facts and processes that are necessary to function in life, stick to the basics, and avoid anything too fancy until learners have mastered this basic information and begin specialized training in vocational or post-secondary academic situations.

However, one may look at curriculum from a number of angles and through a number of lenses, and these points of view generally have the effect of determining the purpose of school. Depending on what group has the power to control the purpose of the educational system, one encounters different emphases, values, and pedagogies.

Typically, and the trend for at least the last decade, has been to see school curriculum through the lens of preparation for the workplace or higher education. These are both worthy objectives. We want each generation to have the skills and knowledge to be productive, contributing members of society. David J. Hoff, in an article about major business organizations' backing of the No Child Left Behind Act (NCLBA) goals says that "All of those efforts have one goal in common: to make American workers of the future economically competitive" (Hoff 2006, 24).

This is not the only lens, though, and perhaps not even the most powerful one to use if the goal is to optimize the educational system.

This book attempts to define basic aspects of the curriculum when viewed through the larger lens of the schools being the principal instrument through which we maintain an effective democracy. In that case, the purpose of education is to prepare our students to take their rightful place as active members of a democracy. This purpose is larger than workplace or college readiness and, in fact, subsumes them.

Simply seeing students as future workers/consumers or future continuing academic students is inevitably reductionist, as it does not consider quality of life in broad terms; a peaceful, participative society; or individual spiritual fulfillment as part of the educational agenda.

The United States is obsessed with one form of competitiveness. That is, we see being in the world as a zero-sum game. We must be the best, by which we mean the biggest, the strongest, the richest, the most powerful, the most influential. It is no surprise that the news of other countries' outscoring us on international exams of academic skills, in particular math skills, is wounding.

As long as we see the world in this way, however, we are always going to be subject to these kinds of wounds. Our typical response to this type of self-esteem loss is to hunker down and get tough. We will work harder, teach more, move faster than the others. This approach worked in World War II and as a response to the Soviet Union's launching of Sputnik, but will it work as well in response to more generalized comparisons, such as who has the best math students or who has the most PhD's?

Other forms of competition are open to us. For instance, the United Nations has rated Norway as the nation with the highest standard of living and as being the world's best place to live for four years in a row. The latest rating had the United Sates in eighth place. How can that be?

The answer is in priorities and who defines them. In this competition, quality of life, life expectancy, literacy, cultural freedom, tolerance, clean water, fresh air as well as wealth were primary factors (Berglund 2004). We are the richest nation in the world, yet many children go to bed hungry, one can see homeless people in most cities, and we do not have universal health care. We don't even have the lowest infant mortality rate. This kind of information leads one to rethink the game we are in, its rules, our responses, and whether we even want to play at all.

To cite another country that has chosen a different standard of quality,

> they, the Danish people, decided to emphasize social harmony, cooperation, and communitarianism, and to reduce the undesirable effects of competition and individualism and greed on their society and on their children. The freedom to be rich and privileged and to exploit those who were less fortunate in their choice of parents had to yield to the right of all members of the society to be treated with respect and dignity. (Morrill 2007, 34)

The current standards movement dates back at least fifteen years, and this effort to define the purpose and content of the best school curriculum has led us to the current climate of accountability and testing. This has not been a sudden shift, but rather a gradual response to what has been seen as the declining effectiveness of our educational system. What has been happening is by no means all bad.

Holding the educational system accountable for its work is a reasonable thing to do. We expect a certain standard of performance from all professionals: doctors, lawyers, psychotherapists, architects. We also expect a certain standard of performance from the trades: mechanics, electricians, plumbers. Asking people to be responsible for what they do is a normal response when we hire someone to provide a service, such as teaching our children. In fact, we can see many ways in which the demand for accountability is long overdue.

Another feature of the standards movement worth a positive note is its having forced us to take a harder look at those students who are not meeting learning expectations: the learning disabled, racial minorities, and children from lower socioeconomic sectors of our community. For instance, "the federal No Child Left Behind Act has prompted a significant improvement in the education of students with disabilities, a panel of education experts told a House subcommittee" (Samuels 2007, 22). Achievement gaps between these kids and their majority peers have persisted for all too long, and now educators have to explain and remedy this situation.

Finally, the educational reform movement has pushed the long-awaited review of the programs that prepare our teachers. Many teachers lament how much they did not learn in teacher education programs, local in-service programs, or continuing education courses. A large and growing body of knowledge about teaching and learning is developing from psychology, brain research, philosophy, business, human development, and the experiences of teachers in the field. We need to get this information into the hands of teachers, especially those who are just being trained to enter the classroom.

While these are worthy goals, some of the solutions being implemented can be not only ineffective but also deleterious to the education of our children, the welfare of our nation, and indeed the well-being of our planet. For example, consider high-stakes testing on a limited range of subjects.

Daily newspapers and other news sources are considered important instructional resources for teaching about citizenship, politics, and government, and many teachers are using the news more now than they did five years ago, according to a recent survey. But testing mandates are making it more difficult for the majority of the social science teachers who responded to the survey to fit current events into the curriculum.

"Although teachers see the news as one of the best ways to get students interested in a class and its subject, and to prepare students for their role as citizens," the report says, "they do not see it as a good way to prepare students for standardized tests." (Manzo 2007, 12)

In what appears to be a typical American solution to these issues, we simply demand more. If we need more mathematicians, then we will literally stuff more information into the math curriculum, demand its attainment by our students, and offer greater support for math and engineering students in colleges and universities.

Alec M. Resnick is a junior majoring in mathematics at the Massachusetts Institute of Technology (MIT). He is also working with the Edgerton Center and Office of Educational Innovation and Technology at MIT. Being in the educational system as it intensifies certain aspects of curriculum and then imposes high-stakes testing, he is able to see it close up.

> He says, "The atmosphere to which this burgeoning culture of omnipresent carrots and sticks is partner suffocates the carefree curiosity that should be the hallmark of a good student. . . . We are spending more time studying more narrowly just to remain competitive. How will it end? . . . In most cases, all [students] have gained is a knowledge of facts, and they have lost confidence in their ability to think, learn, analyze, and absorb unaided." (Resnick 2007, 26–27)

The situation, however, is even more complex than this. One cannot simply legislate that students perform better without rethinking the whole system of education. One thinks of civil rights legislation aimed at helping to integrate multiple races peacefully. Legislating that people not harass one another may curb the harassment, but it does not necessarily change the way people feel about each other. Similarly, making it the law that students attain certain levels of achievement by certain ages cannot change individuals' learning rates or styles.

Telling people how to think and what they should want is, in a way, bordering on the disrespectful. On March 22, 2007, the Colorado house of representatives' education committee rejected a bill that would have followed the lead of several other states in mandating that students take more math and science courses. "I believe in a well-rounded education. Those words don't seem to be in vogue anymore," said Representative Michael Merrifield (Cavanagh 2007, 19). Jane W. Urschel, associate executive director for the Colorado Association of School Boards added,

> that it is just as essential for students to develop "soft skills," in areas such as public speaking and working collaboratively with others, which would be lost as electives were cut." . . . Students are "not all engineers. They may not all want to be engineers," Ms. Urschel said. School board members, she added, "find it offensive that there is an assumption that every kid wants to go to a four-year college, and that there are inferior dreams." (Cavanagh 2007, 21)

Vermont's "Framework of Standards" contains over 150 separate standards, each of which theoretically applies from kindergarten through grade twelve. Can every one of these standards be vital for every child? How can a teacher keep track of 150 standards and the level and content of their specific implementation in each separate year of school?

We have yet to learn that less can be more, although we are beginning to see this truth in some areas. Both the National Council of Teachers of Mathematics and the National Research Council (writing about science education) have called for fewer but more significant educational targets at each grade level (L. Olson 2006, 1). In those countries with better math scores than ours, the textbooks are much slimmer than those found in the United States.

Rather than solving math problems by algorithm, students in these math-excelling countries may actually work on only one problem in a week. They might work in groups, experimenting with various approaches to the problem, bringing their previous knowledge to bear on finding a solution. They learn to think mathematically; they become mathematicians.

If we continue responding to the crisis in education with the typical, competitive attitude that more and bigger are better, we then simply build a curriculum that overwhelms the system.

> "Everyone recognizes that we can't keep trying to do what we do now," agreed Robert J. Marzano, a senior scholar at Mid-continental Research for Education and Learning, the federally financed regional laboratory in Denver. "It's too much. We have to race through stuff in the name of coverage. . . . When you get committees representing subject areas at a state or national level, it's impossible," he said. "If I'm representing science, I don't want to leave anything out." (L. Olson 2006, 15)

We know that students learn in many different ways and at varying rates. When we fail to acknowledge this idea, visiting assistant professor of education at Wheaton College Kirsten Olson (2006, 29) reported that students told her that "school fractured what they feel are their deepest strengths: their creativity, their humanity, and their capacity to imagine" (K. Olson 2006, p. 29).

Why then do we write standards that we attach to specific grade levels and that are tested on a met-the-standard or did-not-meet-the-standard basis? Wouldn't a true standards-based system vary the time line, with some students reaching the standard earlier than the average student and others later? The goals of education should define what constitutes a basic education, not necessarily how long it takes to attain it. Education does not have to be a race, nor does it have to be a competition. As Robert Epstein, former editor in chief of *Psychology Today* and a contributing editor to *Scientific American*, reminds us,

> people have radically different learning styles and abilities, and effective learning—learning that benefits *all* students—is necessarily individualized and

self-paced. . . . In today's fast-paced world, education needs to be spread out over a lifetime, and the main thing we need to teach our young people is to love the process of learning. (Epstein 2007, 28)

In addressing this issue of pace, New York state's deputy education commissioner overseeing individuals with disabilities told a house subcommittee that we should allow for students who can learn subjects to the same breadth and depth as their peers but who learn more slowly (Samuels 2007, 22). Expecting all students to reach the same point at the same time is plainly educationally unsound and has led to a culture of high-stakes testing.

What gets tested gets taught, especially if the law imposes sanctions on schools whose students do not perform well on the test. The results are not necessarily advantageous to the educational system or to the students. David C. Berliner, Regents' professor of education at Arizona State University, and Sharon L. Nicholas, assistant professor of educational psychology at the University of Texas, write that

> by restricting the education of our young people and substituting for it training for performing well on high-stakes examinations, we are turning America into a nation of test-takers, abandoning our heritage as a nation of thinkers, dreamers, and doers. (Berliner and Nichols 2007, 36)

This culture of high-stakes testing has also altered the way in which some teachers see their students. According to one Florida superintendent,

> "When a low-performing child walks into a classroom, instead of being seen as a challenge, or an opportunity for improvement, for the first time since I've been in education, teachers are seeing [that child] as a liability." (Berliner and Nichols 2007, 36)

Linking the purpose of education to economic success and competitiveness in the world market has reached levels of obsession and even absurdity. Children are reduced from human beings bursting with all sorts of potential to objects of economic success when organizations, such as the Partners for America's Economic Success, offer the philosophy, as summarized by Robert Dugger, that, "Educating children in their earliest years is not only a moral imperative . . . but also a sound economic investment that will yield a healthy rate of return" (Borja 2007a, 12).

Using the phrases "moral imperative" and "healthy rate of return" in the same sentence leaves one with an eerie feeling. At the annual conference of the Committee for Economic Development, presenters suggested that "providing a sound and academically rigorous education to the nation's youngest children is among the most effective ways to ensure they become productive workers and citizens in adulthood" (Borja 2007a, 12). What is meant here by the word *citizens*?

Have we come to a point where we see the purpose of education as manufacturing cogs for an economic machine? A paper issued by two senior fellows of the Brookings Institution, Jens Ludwig and Isabel V. Sawhill, makes the point that research has shown that educating children as early as four months of age through an academically rigorous curriculum improves their job opportunities later in life" (Borja 2007b, 7).

Apparently, according to this economic or business point of view, the primary purpose of schools is to mold students into the most productive and competitive workers possible for our nation's future economic gain. If this were indeed the number one purpose of our educational system, it would reflect a limited world view of material acquisition and power.

> Jeffery Miller, a youth-development consultant, reminds us that amid calls for a dramatic overhaul of American education aimed at preserving the nation's dominant position in the global community, there are still voices advocating more-traditional ideals of education, such as preparation for living in and passing on a democracy (Miller 2007, 36).

Nell Noddings has written passionately that there is more to school than job preparation. "The school must do more by way of educating than mere job preparation" (Noddings 2005a, 72). She argues that schools have many purposes that supersede workforce preparation. She says

> My alternative vision suggests an entirely different organization of schooling. One can only speculate on what the disciplines might have been and how the curriculum would have been constructed if, for example, women instead of men had designed them. Women have traditionally been closer to the everyday cares of life, but their subordination to men has generated twin problems: First, women have not had the power to enact ideas that were generated by traditional female values; second, attributes, values, and tasks associated with women have been systematically devalued—even scorned. If it were possible to redesign education along the lines of our alternative vision, we would see children studying, discussing, exploring matters, and doing things in their various centers of care. Teachers would work with all children on topics of general concern and with small groups of children on more specialized subjects. (61)

As far as preparation for the workplace, Noddings envisioned the following:

> The presence of caring adults in regular conversation can assure them [students] that there are many ways to earn a respectable living and contribute to the community; that there is a place for them in the community now and in the future; and that we all recognize the continuity of purpose that guides both the school and the community. (66)

This brings us to my view on the primary purpose of the American public school. As reported by the Washington-based Center on Education Policy, "public schools play a vital role in promoting the common good in American society" (*Education Week* 2007a, 13). Among those values cited by the Center are "unifying a diverse population, *preparing students for citizenship in a democratic society* [emphasis added], ensuring equality for all children, and teaching students to be economically self-sufficient" (*Education Week* 2007a, 13). According to the report "Why We Still Need Public Schools: Public Education for the Common Good," all of the public school goals listed above coincide with the betterment of society (Kober 2007).

Thus, the overarching goal of the public school, as argued in this book, is the preparation of our students to take their rightful places in a democratic society. This does not exclude other goals; as Noddings has written schools have multiple goals (Noddings 2005a). However, preparing students to be active members of a fully functioning democracy subsumes such goals as workforce preparedness and developing an intellectual base in students for further academic pursuits.

If we are serious about being a democracy, our society requires some specific educational foci for our schools. Above all, a democracy demands an educated, involved populace to function. We cannot allow our political debates to deteriorate into competing sound bites. We cannot allow productive discussion to become instead immovable ideologies incapable of merging through dialogue, compromise, and consensus into the best solutions to our problems.

We have to live together in respect and mutual care. We have to be able to understand and respond to the complex situations of contemporary life. Our schools' purpose should be to prepare students to perform these vital tasks and take these vital roles as members of the greatest democracy in the world.

> The 2003 report "The Civic Mission of School," published by the Carnegie Corporation of New York and the Center for Information and Research on Civic Learning and Engagement, offers six promising approaches to civic learning. These include instruction in government, history, law, and democracy; classroom discussions of current events and issues; service learning; extracurricular activities that provide opportunities for students to get involved in their communities; opportunities for student participation in classroom and school governance; and simulations of democratic processes. (Miller 2007, 36)

A democracy is a government for the people and by the people. We are acknowledging that when we finally pay proper attention to those segments of our society who have been left behind. We are acknowledging that when we try to bring all students up to high standards of performance. And finally, by holding the educational system accountable, we are demanding the preparation of citizens who are up to the task of democratic involvement.

The question remains, however, how to do this—and what happens to this worthy goal if we do not see it as the primary purpose of schools but, instead, as secondary to economic goals. In most of the material referenced above, *citizenship*, defined clearly as active membership in a participatory government, has not been defined, if mentioned at all, as a primary element of what our schools should be doing.

This book posits four major starting points for education under the purpose of preparing students for functional membership in a democracy: kindness, thinking, problem solving, and communications. These four foundational elements should be taught in every class, at every level, every day. They form the backbone of a great educational system.

Rather than start with our current standards, which are subject-driven, atomized lists of facts and skills, too extensive ever to be completed, I suggest that we start with the broad foundation pieces, the pieces that cut across individual subject areas and provide the basis for well-rounded, self-sufficient, and well-educated human and humane beings.

Let us begin with kindness. While without a doubt, many people exhibit kindness, we also see the lack of kindness all around us. We just have to watch some of the "news" talk shows on television or listen to them on the radio. Individual shows take a point of view, say conservative or liberal, and spend their time bashing the other side.

People enter the discussion with minds made up and leave the discussion feeling the same as when they entered. Without kindness, no listening, no appreciation of the other's point of view, and certainly no combining of ideas into larger and more powerful models representing the best of both sides can occur. How can a democracy survive without meaningful debate?

Furthermore, kindness can work against hegemony. In our case the reduction of hegemony is essential if we are to perform productively in the world marketplace. We will have to withhold judgment of others in an attempt to understand and respect the various cultures around the world. There is no right or wrong here, but a multiplicity of views and customs define the world.

With kindness, we can come together. Without it, understanding is difficult at best, and conflict is likely. The plethora of programs designed to teach students anger management skills, empathy, and conflict resolution techniques is ample evidence that we are not all born with kindness built in. Our schools must help students learn the social skills that they have not acquired naturally.

The examples that follow are true. A student throws pennies at a Jewish high school teacher and demands, "Dance for pennies." A parent comes to school and harasses a teacher who uses a spelling game that plays on the pun of *spell* as orthography and *spell* as a magical incantation. A kindergarten teacher has a young boy standing in front of the class who had failed to use the bathroom during the designated time. Now, holding his crotch in a desperate attempt not to soil himself, he strains as the teacher publicly berates him before allowing him to use the toilet.

How can we ever become a democratic nation if we allow people to treat each other in this way? Kindness is not respect. Kindness is truly caring about others, attempting to understand them, and coming together peacefully. One of the foundations of democracy is people working together for the benefit of everyone.

We must listen to each other, respect each other, and come together because, as the saying goes, *"e pluribus unum."* We cannot expect students to learn, to take risks, to try new things if they are in fear of embarrassment, bullying, or being different. Ironically, often the very best students in advanced classes do not answer questions for fear of being wrong. Without risks and mistakes, there is no learning. Without caring and unity, there can be only limited democracy.

Next, we have to teach our students how to think. Courses in rhetoric, logic, and debate have all but disappeared. An individual, a family, a nation all situations requiring thinking through complexities. As our students listen to political speeches, are they able to understand the logic of the arguments presented? Can they see the sequential or logical flaws? Do they understand the logic of cause and effect?

The lack of these skills can lead to some frightening consequences. When we do not think a situation through to its logical conclusions, we can often miss unanticipated results. For instance, the current federal education law declares that all students meet the standard by the year 2014. But as worthy a goal as this is, doesn't simple statistical reality tell us that 100 percent attainment is not possible due to natural fluctuation and variance? We do not want members of a democracy voting based on emotions (the politics of fear), prejudice, or the good looks of the presenter.

One theory about Richard Nixon's losing the first televised presidential debates to John Kennedy was that Nixon did not understand the new medium, he did not look into the camera enough, and his makeup was not as effective as that of Kennedy. Much was made of George Bush's looking at his watch during the debate with Bill Clinton. The fate of the nation, and perhaps the world, should turn on what a candidate has to say, not how the candidate looks or sounds.

On the other side, we want our students to be able to build arguments that can withstand examination. Letters to the editor, presentations at school board meetings, or responses at local political meetings all come to mind. Here we also see the return of kindness, as people learn to listen to each other carefully and offer and accept criticism in the cause of seeking the best course of action.

The ability to think is the ability to use one's mind. One has to see the various sides of an argument and follow different lines of thought to their conclusions. Are short-term financial gains justification for long-term environmental degradation? Is allowing yourself to strike out at a good friend worth losing that friend forever? Which do we need more, the trees on the hillside, which hold back erosion, or the jobs provided to the forestry industry in an impoverished community?

Debate, weighing options, and understanding and building arguments are at the heart of a democracy. Our goal is to provide our students with the necessary skills to look at all the options, to compare their relative strengths and weaknesses, to pick up obvious logical flaws, to understand the arguments of another, and to prepare cogent arguments themselves.

Thinking is clearly as much a social skill as anything else. Diplomacy depends on thinking through situations, understanding, seeing connections, and ultimately finding a path to peaceful solutions that provide the most benefit for the most people. This applies as well on the playground as it does in the United Nations. In our classrooms, we must take every opportunity to ask students to explain their thinking and the thinking of others in order to give them practice in this skill. We must not fear criticism but welcome it as constructive adjustment to faulty thinking. We need to foster the habit of asking clarifying questions to ensure sound thinking and understanding.

The third foundational skill is the logical extension of thinking to problem solving. We are often stuck in believing that problem solving is a math or science issue, but that is not the case. All aspects of life involve problem solving, and in a democracy, the people are supposed to solve problems, either directly or through their elected leaders.

When the family consumer science teacher asks the class to take a recipe for one and turn it into a recipe for twenty, he has posed a problem. When the physical education teacher asks how to deal with a zone defense in basketball, she has posed a problem. When a nation is devastated by flood, other nations have to organize and develop solutions to problems of supply collection, movement, and delivery—massive logistics problems. On the playground, students have to resolve conflicts or, in other words, solve problems. As teachers and other adults, our job is to model these behaviors for young people.

Clearly, kindness, thinking, and problem solving all relate to and reinforce one another. Tying them all together is the final foundational skill, communication. We live in a world of extremely complex communication, the giving and receiving of information. If we could not communicate, then we could not live in a democracy. In fact, no community could develop at all. The most immediate way to think of communication is to consider the four standard functions taught in English class: reading, writing, speaking, and listening.

However, these four activities are merely the beginning. Their equivalent exists in hundreds of foreign languages, for instance. We can look at musical notation, scientific notation, and mathematics each as a separate form of communication. Computer languages abound. People share ideas through sign language and signal systems made from flags or smoke. We communicate through body position, facial expression, gestures, tone of voice, cadence, and volume.

A world of difference resides in a sentence delivered by someone looking straight into your eyes and the same words said by someone looking at the floor. In ancient India, the reversed swastika was a religious symbol. If one were to use it today, it would be seen as a representation of hate, intolerance, and fascism. Imagine the miscommunication that a lack of this knowledge might cause!

Understanding what others have to say to us and making ourselves understood to others may be the single most important aspect of the communal life of human beings, making that life possible. Ideas that cannot be transferred from one person to another die with their creator. One easily sees how communication underlies and is the most powerful of the four curriculum foundations. People need to listen to each other, either verbally or nonverbally, with kindness. They need to understand and be understood. Finally, they will have to work together to solve the problems we all face.

The argument of this book is to see the purpose of school as the preparation of students to be fully vested members of a democratic society. Rather than begin with the atomization of the standard academic disciplines, I prefer to start with the big, foundational cornerstones. A presenter once placed a large glass jar before her audience and filled it with large rocks. She asked if it were full. The answer, or course, was no, since there was so much air space in the jar. She then added gravel to the jar and asked the same question. This led to adding sand to the jar. Finally, she added water to the jar, and then it was full. The lesson, she said, was to put in the big rocks first.

We must put in the big rocks first. The rest follows. If students understand kindness, thinking, problem solving, and communicating, do you not think that they then can learn whatever else they find necessary for a fulfilled and quality life?

But without these four factors, we run the risk of developing walking encyclopedias out of our students; creating cogs for the workforce; and neglecting the spiritual, moral, and loving aspects of their natures. They may excel at producing and consuming, but will they be happy, contributing, and empowered members of a democracy?

A report financed by the William T. Grant Foundation and published in the *American Educational Research Journal* finds that "High school students who take part in community service, both voluntarily and to fulfill a school requirement, are more likely than peers who weren't participants to vote and volunteer as adults" (*Education Week* 2007b, 14).

This book does not presume to be the final word on any of the topics of curriculum. It does, however, insist that more aspects than those prevailing gain a full voice in the debate. Public school educators, parents, and politicians often do not have the time to read the professional literature on education. We get our news from the television, radio, and newspapers.

The attempt here is to bridge the gap, at least a little, between what scholars, high-powered think tanks, political leaders, and businesses are saying about education and what is happening on the ground, in classrooms and communities. If this book can do that, bring the general public into the educational reform debate from a more informed position and provide a responding voice to the powerful direction in which our educational system is moving, then it will have accomplished its purpose.

Fifty years ago, the British educator Molly Brearly described the basics of education as follows:

"The main work of the school is surely the fostering and developing of mental life, enabling children to experience more fully and consciously all that life has to offer. This large, overall aim is to be achieved by an infinity of small steps. The material we provide children can seldom be thought of as an end in itself, but rather as a means through which effective thinking and feeling are fostered." (O'Brien 2007, 31)

Let's take another look at our educational system, and this time, let's consider preparing the next generation of citizens for a democratic society as its primary purpose.

1

Curriculum at the Level of Survival: What Is the Purpose of Education?

Standards and testing have come to dominate the national and local educational landscape. There has been a rush to judgment about our schools, our teachers, and our methods in this country. What I see as a need is to go deeper in the debate, to go beyond listing more and more topics and skills to teach and test. Many books explain procedural knowledge, such as how to differentiate instruction, or how to create a standards-based curriculum, or how to write a constructivist lesson. However, I want to discuss the *what* and *why* rather than the *how*.

What exactly is the purpose of schools in a free, democratic society, and why is the answer to that question crucial in deciding the most fundamental questions about curriculum? The need to examine these questions is necessary because without them, as I think we can already see, schools may move in the wrong direction, narrowing curricula to comply with political and economic agendas, in the end actually producing individuals less suited for life in a democracy and worldwide economic competition.

I am encountering an increasing number of voices opposed to what is happening in education, and this book would help frame the current educational debate through the lenses of curriculum, democracy, and more effective strategies of accountability.

PREPARING THE WORKFORCE

A key cliché and danger sign is the discussion of schools as the sources of qualified members of the workforce. This is a very limited and worrisome vision of the future of our current generation. Wouldn't it make more sense to see our children as future members of a truly democratic society, devoted to the principles of the United States Constitution? If we could do that, I believe that the superior workforce would follow as a corollary, but not the other way around.

In addition, whenever I hear education and the economy linked as part of a political agenda, red lights begin to flash. Too often, this means the limited view of schools as institutions whose primary responsibility is to supply foot soldiers for the workplace. "Governor Taft, often aligned with business leaders in his state, said that high school reform is an issue of economics in Ohio. "The preparation of our workforce is probably the number-one issue in Ohio'" (Richard 2004, 8). The February 2, 2005, edition of *Education Week* has no fewer than three articles on this theme.

PUTTING FIRST THINGS FIRST

My concerns here are many, but they fall primarily into one major category with four parts: put first-things-first back into the curriculum. We need to get back to the precurriculum issues and start with the overarching scaffold of kindness, communication, problem solving, and thinking.

These four factors can and should provide the foundation for all education in every classroom in every lesson. These form the backbone of a solid, humane education, which has as its goals sensitive, insightful, intelligent human beings capable of operating successfully within the kind of collective democracy that we like to talk about, the ideal vision of the United States of America and, hopefully, the world. We should be holding our educational system accountable for producing students who meet that description.

We want Americans to be whole people, people who care about their environment, each other, and the world. We want them to be able to enter into the dialogue of great ideas, to enter into the life of the mind. We want them to be healthy and happy. We want a strong America that is respected throughout the world, not just for its military and economic might but also for the richness of its people's spirits and values.

See what happens when we return to the one role of education as preparing the workforce when we look through these four new lenses and listen to the words of Ed Simon, president of Herman Miller Corporation, quoted in Peter Senge's *The Fifth Discipline.*

"Why can't work be one of those wonderful things in life? Why can't we cherish and praise it, versus seeing work as a necessity? Why can't it be a cornerstone in people's lifelong process of developing ethics, values, and in expressing the humanities and the arts? Why can't people learn through the process

that there's something about the beauties of design, of building something to
last, something of value? I believe that this potential is inherent in work, more
so than in many other places." (Senge 1990, 144)

A STRONG AND HEALTHY AMERICA

Now more than ever, exactly when we seem to be seeing education in simplistic and reductionist terms, we must return to the cliché of educating the
whole child, ensuring that it is not a cliché at all but a reality and a highly
valued goal. One of the best aspects of the current view of education is that
we can no longer fail to address the learning gaps between rich and poor,
minority and majority, regular and disabled students. We are finally taking
a hard look at how we prepare our teaching force; holding teacher preparation institutions and teachers themselves accountable is long overdue. My
concern is that we are not holding education accountable for the most important results or in a logical, productive manner.

And if we really are serious about preparing the workforce, shouldn't we
be taking into account its health as well as its ability to engage in productivity? I have been reading a fair amount about the physical condition of
Americans, especially those in our schools. However, physical education is
not a core subject according to the federal government; therefore, Title II
money (part of the Consolidated Federal Programs grant money earmarked
for professional development) cannot be used to enhance the skills of physical education teachers, or even health teachers for that matter.

John P. Allegrante, professor of health education at Teachers College, Columbia University, tells us that "growing evidence suggests that the nation's
health and education goals are inextricably linked: Students with health problems simply aren't as ready or as capable to learn" (Allegrante 2004, 38).

Why would we not want to put emphasis on student health? Employers
balk at providing health care to their employees because of the prohibitive
costs of insurance, resulting in the embarrassment that so many people are
without health coverage in the richest nation in the world. Wouldn't industry want a healthier workforce, which would not only bring down the cost
of insurance and prescription drugs but also reduce the number of sick
days, boost productivity, and the purchase of leisure time goods and services? This is just one example of where the educational reform movement,
despite having its heart in the right place, is missing the bigger picture.

Another cliché comes to mind, something about what one learns on the
playing fields of Eton. An emphasis on team sports, not even necessarily competitive sports, would support not only health but also teamwork, collaboration, selflessness, a sense of purpose, and generally supportive behaviors. In
fact, athletic teams have to solve a lot of problems. Individuals must take on

various leadership roles and share their talents. Think of the kinds of activities one encounters on ropes courses, for instance. These activities are physically, mentally, and socially challenging. Physical education could be a centerpiece of our educational system.

EDUCATING THE WHOLE CHILD

"Educating the whole child" is one of those clichés that is impossible to oppose. Of course, we want all of our children to be healthy in body, mind, and spirit. However, too often, the phrase is hollow as we focus only on the mind, and even then on only narrow portions of the mind. The current educational reform movement, with its concrete and limited view of education, only exacerbates this problem. Yale professor Robert J. Sternberg writes,

> Schooling is more and more emphasizing the traditional three R's of reading, writing, and arithmetic . . . but they are not all that matters to a sound education. Children, more and more, are being deprived of learning in art, music, history and social science, physical education, special programs for the gifted, and the like. In general, anything that might enrich children's education in a way that would make the children knowledgeable as well as wise and ready to make complex decisions in today's complex world is largely gone (Sternberg 2004, 56).

Bruce G. Hammond sums up the current educational testing situation neatly when he says, "As standardized testing advances from all directions, teachers and administrators face a momentous choice: Are we mainly concerned with educating our students, or with ranking them?" (Hammond 2005, 32).

Now, more than ever, we need the concept of the whole child to be more than a cliché. As educators, we have an ethical obligation to prevent the erosion of the educational system into a testing machine designed to manufacture potential employees. Typically, this narrow view of schools translates into teaching students how to read, write, and calculate. Often lost are creativity, social skills, collaboration skills, appreciation of what is read and seen on a level beyond simple understanding, spiritual growth, physical well-being, and cultural open-mindedness.

According to Gerald W. Bracey, "only the foolish would think that 13-year-olds' skills at bubbling in answer sheets would mean much for a nation's well-being" (Bracey 2005, 38). Terry Roberts, director of the National Paideia Center, warns us that

> perhaps the most disturbing of all, we have narrowed our teaching focus to those skills that can be measured with a multiple-choice question or, at most,

a brief essay. I am awfully afraid that what we now term "high-stakes account-ability" has squeezed wonder out of the classroom. (2004, 31)

A ROLE FOR THE ARTS IN DEMOCRACY

Preparing students to be members of the workforce is a worthy ambition, but it should be a subset of the larger role of schools, which is to prepare students for a fulfilling and productive life. Another cliché that arises here is that we need to educate our children to be capable of playing a role in a democratic society. This means having the ability to understand and build an argument, to be aware of crucial issues all around us, to take citizenship seriously, and to care about more than oneself. "As an ideal, democracy assumes the capacity of the common person to learn, to think independently, to decide thoughtfully" (Rose 2005, 41).

I am not seeing too much about these issues in the debate about our nation's school curricula, yet according to former Secretary of Education Rod Paige and Arkansas Governor Mike Huckabee, "as a nation, we must develop children who are productive, happy, well-adjusted citizens, rather than kids who can just pass a test and get through school" (Paige and Huckabee 2005, 52).

In fact, if the Bush administration itself stands as a model, then one should make a decision and stick with it regardless of any new information or contradictory findings that may turn up along the way. Hollow words and clichés beget mixed messages and confusion. Accountability is crucial, but that does not mean that we should be afraid to teach subjects that are difficult to measure

Seeing schools as workforce factories is also ironic. The engines of industry are asking for workers who are creative, can lead, can deal with ambiguity, can solve problems, and can work in collaborative groups. Where in a school would one learn these skills? One clear answer is through the arts, literature, drama, math that goes beyond the memorization of algorithms, and the social sciences. Yet Sandra Stotsky, research scholar at Northeastern University, points out that

> most states provide absolutely no content-rich literature standards and/or selective reading lists to outline the substantive content of the high school English curriculum. Indeed, the study of American literature by name is not required in about half the states, and the two-word phrase is barely mentioned in many others. . . . It is much easier to emphasize informational and practical reading on a state test than to try to figure out what is being taught in the English class (2004, 30).

The law demands testing in math, reading, and perhaps writing. Science is in the wings. Yet another cliché, what gets tested gets taught, applies here.

Forget about the social sciences. We can talk about the arts, but do we mean it?

EDUCATIONAL SCAFFOLDING

The idea of "scaffolding" is not new to education. Even before the word was applied to the classroom, good teachers were giving students the necessary supports to hold them up as they reached for ever more sophisticated concepts, skills, and understandings. Words that come up in the dictionary under *"scaffold"* are *"temporary," "movable," "supporting,"* and *"framework."* In the same way that a construction scaffold allows people to work on a building, an educational scaffold supports students as they take initial, uncertain steps to advance their learning.

Scaffolds are movable and temporary, implying that the worker or student is progressing so that the level of the scaffold has to move with the work. The scaffold also holds up the partial building while other parts are completed. In education, that means holding up students as they work their way through new knowledge, a piece at a time, until all the pieces come together.

The concept is simple. The application can be quite complex. In a class of twenty students, all at slightly different levels while trying to learn how to perform double-digit division, several scaffolds may be needed at any one time. Blocks, times tables, verbal explanations, hints, and connections to earlier and simpler problems all provide support for the student struggling to understand and master the new concept and process. Props for verbal, kinesthetic, and visual learners apply to the scaffolding for different students learning the same thing. Even tying lessons to various student interests can provide a kind of scaffold, keeping the student attached to the work at hand.

Scaffolding has been discussed as a deep, complex process in cognitive psychology. Here, scholars examine the concept of scaffolding, not specific scaffolds. Thus, the question arises: "Is there the possibility of a kind of generic scaffold, a scaffold that should underpin all of curriculum, all teaching and learning?"

This would be a scaffold within which the subject-specific and student-specific scaffolds would stand. Such a scaffold would define the most fundamental characteristics of a curriculum, since it would "hold up" everything else. It would define the most basic teaching and learning, the primary knowledge and skills necessary to support any excellent curriculum. In other words, what is the necessary underpinning for a humane education with the goal of helping people become productive members of a collaborative world community?

In the current frenzy to define outcomes and standards, to test students, to make sure that they can read, write, and compute, we may very well be missing the point of a good education despite the best of intentions, held in place by the super-scaffold of values and skills that one needs to participate fully in a democracy.

For instance, we may teach students to "read" in the sense of decoding. The reader can stand before a group, book in hand, and pronounce each word correctly in sequence as it is written on the page. Is that reading? The same student may be able to compute the answers to one hundred multiplication problems efficiently and accurately. Is that mathematics?

One cannot dispute that skills and information are primary aspects of any education. However, if we do not also engage students in the processes of using those skills and knowledge for greater purposes than demonstrating their proficiency at knowing them, we have woefully failed as educators. We have known for centuries that knowledge is power and, in particular, a well-informed and educated people is necessary for a successful democracy. One simply has to examine the use of propaganda and control of information throughout history to see the validity of this point.

THE CURRICULUM OF TRIVIAL PURSUIT

In a recent *Education Week* commentary, Ernest Boyer's son Paul laments that his father's predictions about curriculum and testing are coming true:

> Testing, as it is now implemented, acts as a powerful current, pulling American education not toward coherence, but toward a constricted and fragmented curriculum. By focusing with the intensity of a laser beam on the test scores and narrow, short-term strategies to raise them, the deeper purpose of education is cast in shadows and slowly forgotten. (Boyer 2005, 41)

The elder Boyer called such "academic rigor, when detached from any larger educational purpose 'an exercise in trivial pursuit'" (Boyer 2005, 40).

THE SUPER SCAFFOLD

Now, our nation is scurrying to meet standards. Many of those standards focus on reading, writing, and mathematics as skills to be mastered. This does not lead to the educated populace we so desperately need to maintain our democracy. We are missing the point, which is to help students use the skills, knowledge, and processes that they are learning.

Imagine a citizen reading the daily newspaper, understanding every word of an article on pollutants in the atmosphere. Now imagine that he is incapable of forming an opinion based on the information, generating a hypothesis, writing a response, or discussing the issue. He can read. Or can he?

What is the scaffold within which an ideal curriculum exists? What are the overarching concepts and skills that form the bedrock and support of an excellent education? If they are not basic skills but, in fact, something that actually precedes basic skills and then follows educational development for life, they must be powerful indeed. I would like to suggest again that four such pillars comprise the super-scaffold: kindness, thinking, problem solving, and communication.

As we examine these four elements of the super-scaffold, they may bear a resemblance to many other concepts. I am not suggesting that these are the only or even best names to use for these concepts. What each of these words represents is the issue, not the words themselves.

Kindness

Beginning with kindness, we examine how this simple term can be applied in innumerable ways to every lesson at every age level. For instance, some current issues in schools involve violence, bullying, harassment, teasing, and vandalism. Think about the culture of hazing among athletes. How can we expect students to learn at peak levels under these circumstances?

We need to consider what an atmosphere of fear or discomfort does to a student physically as well as psychological. Can we expect someone to take risks, to hypothesize, to take an educated guess at an answer if classmates laugh when someone is wrong? Do we honor all responses and attempts? Can optimal learning occur within an environment of stress, including the stress of having to score well on the prescribed examination?

Kindness incorporates respect for everyone: students, teachers, administrators, support staff, parents, board members, other community members. A series of papers by a group of researchers, educators, and government leaders called the "Wingspread Declaration" lists the following suggestions for improving school environments:

> "setting high academic expectations; applying fair and consistent discipline policies; fostering trusting relationships among students, teachers, administrators, and families; ensuring that a supportive adult watches over every student; creating small learning environments; and even reducing lunchroom noise levels" (Viadero 2004, 10).

Meaningful debate and legitimate argumentation have little chance if some voices are allowed to drown out others, if some opinions are privileged, if people do not feel safe. To learn often means to take risks, to try something new. Learning involves guessing, trial and error, discussion, sharing points of view. Creativity does not thrive in an atmosphere of self-consciousness bred of fear that others will jeer. The current goal to close the various achievement gaps in our society needs to be extended specifically to include giving students the tools necessary to participate in society.

In her 1997 book, *Just Girls: Hidden Literacies and Life in Junior High,* Margaret J. Finders discovered highly complex yet subtle methods by which adolescent girls created and maintained social hierarchies in classrooms and schools.

> The discourse currently circulating around student-centered pedagogy denies the power of the peer dynamic. Students' performances within the classroom cannot be free from sociopolitical tangles. "Free choices" are not free from the webs of social relationships. Students' selections are tied to their social relationships and filtered through their cultural assumptions of appropriate social roles. Since learning is enmeshed in social webs, I argue that a student-centered curriculum must consider the tangles that constrict students' performances. (5)

We need to help students see beyond these social entanglements so that the classroom becomes a place free of threat and anxiety. The first order of business is for everyone to treat everyone else with kindness. Such a concept has reverberations far beyond the classroom, all the way to international relations. We should be teaching our new citizens that they are citizens not only of the United States but also of the world.

The events of the last several years should have taught us that we need to do a better job with helping students to be open and respectful to cultures other than their own. If we disregard or, by inference, degrade the cultures of those unlike us, we then continue to see that some other countries, cultures, or societies perceive us as egocentric, insensitive, belligerent, arrogant, and threatening. Do they hate freedom, as we are told, or do they in fact hate being seen as the second tier of humanity?

Recently, a school system found itself in the unique position of actually having the opportunity to add a language to its foreign language offerings. One would think that a critical language would be the prudent choice, something like Chinese, Arabic, or Japanese (assuming that Spanish was already part of the curriculum).

However, this school chose to offer Italian. There is nothing wrong with Italian. In fact, it is a beautiful language and the source of some of the world's most profound and magnificent literature. However, this once again underscores our Eurocentrism. The choice came as a result of a survey of 307 students and 764 parents. The results were 21 percent opting for Italian, 14 percent for Arabic and Japanese, and 12 percent for Chinese (Bahrampour 2005).

The fact that the choice was in part the result of a popularity contest is disturbing enough, but that our educational system is producing students who do not understand what is happening in the world, and therefore made this choice, is even worse. We cannot afford to ignore developing cultural understanding of the peoples of the Middle East. We cannot afford to ignore developing communication skills with the largest emerging economy in the world, the 1.2 billion inhabitants of China.

While NCLBA does include foreign language in the core subjects, the government has been slow to apply any pressure or monetary incentive to adding critical languages to the curriculum. This kind of approach, egocentric and dismissive, is largely what has landed us in some of our current predicaments. We need to change the way we think as educators and as a nation. If the national leadership does not make these adjustments, then we, as educators, must take an active role. To be sadly blunt about it, kindness and respect for others are in our own best interest. We must indeed educate the whole child.

Thinking

The next pillar is thinking. We can teach our students how to think. Clear, deep thinking does not necessarily come naturally without some nurturing. I once knew an English teacher who asked his Advanced Placement students to match characters and authors with works of literature as part of the final examination. I never understood the point of this exercise in a class that in theory was devoted to a deep understanding of literature. Asking students to think would have been dealing with a more transferable skill.

I once heard a supervisor say that a teacher should never ask a question to which he did not know the answer. To me, that sounded the death knell to interesting classroom conversation. No community of learners, which includes the teacher, exists in that statement. To return to Ernest Boyer for a moment:

> The most meaningful education revealed connections between subjects, between people, and between cultures. '"To be truly educated means going beyond the isolated facts, putting learning in a larger context and, above all, it means discovering the connectedness of things'." (Boyer 2005, 40)

We can help students understand their own thinking through the use of metacognition. To understand how one's thinking works is to begin to gain control of it. Rather than approaching an issue blindly, a student could choose the appropriate, or an appropriate, style of thinking in her attempt to understand the situation. Is this a situation for analysis or synthesis? Would making connections with other knowledge help, or would cause and effect be most useful in gaining understanding? What about a combination of several thinking modes?

What topic, subject, or situation would not be suitable grist for the thinking mill? Looking for connections, relationships, differences: these are means by which we study and come to understand our world.

The person reading the newspaper article on pollutants in the atmosphere should be able to understand the causes and effects of pollution and the reasoning behind various responses to the situation. Then, he should be able to evaluate those responses, make a decision on which makes the most sense to him, or even to create a response of his own. Don't we need deep levels of thinking to respond to a social issue, a work of art, or why the soufflé did not rise?

Kindness and thinking naturally go together. Clear thinking is not likely if the ambiance is one of fear, shame, or self-consciousness. For thinking to flourish, the thinker must know that others accept various thoughts with open minds. The thinker needs to know that the critique from others is not an attack but rather a thoughtful response, which moves the ideas along to ever more sophisticated levels, to a solution, or to the revelation of a logical flaw.

This is learning. This is the business of a community of thinkers in an open society, collaboratively groping for understanding. This is not a test of phonics or multiplication, because even these basic skills would be difficult to learn in an unfriendly, closed environment.

Problem Solving

Knowing how to think and being a part of a respectful learning environment lead to the next pillar: problem solving. The environment allows for the free exchange of ideas, for creativity, for speculation, and for experimentation. Within this atmosphere, an individual or group is free to apply thinking skills to situations needing solutions. All discipline areas at all ages embody problem-solving activity.

Something as simple as deciding what color of beads you want to string could provide an introduction to problem-solving ideas. First, what do you want to make: a bracelet, a necklace, something to hang a key on? Then there are several colors to choose among. What method will you use to choose (favorite color, somebody else's favorite color, to create a design, random selection)?

This is not to suggest that you would necessarily use this terminology with four-year-olds, but you might make them aware of the reasons for their selection by asking them. How will you string the beads: needle, using only the string, using some other tool? This may sound a bit forced, but the point is that one can conceive of the bead-stringing activity as a problem to solve. Given these various beads, string, needles, and other tools perhaps, you are to make a gift for someone. What will you make, how will you make it, and why will you make it the way you do?

Problem solving also allows for reflection, perhaps one of the most important characteristics of a thoughtful, well-educated person. Reflection allows a person to evaluate the work or action. Could I have done that a different way? Is there a better way to do what I have just done? Does this problem remind me of another problem I have already seen or solved? How can I improve on my work?

We know that many connections exist between studying the arts and improvement in traditional academic areas. The arts can also provide opportunities to solve problems. What would be the most effective wording for a poem? Which material best suits my artistic purposes? The arts help to create whole people, not workers who have no lives outside of their jobs. The arts renew and refresh us as well as sharpen our skills. They provide us with an interesting opportunity to study the cultures and values of various peoples.

Stanford University education professor Elliot Eisner argues for inclusion of the arts in his 2004 book, *The Arts and the Creation of Mind*. According to an *Education Week* article, "Eisner argues that including the arts in the curriculum is critically important to the development of thinking skills and a better understanding of the world" (Bradley 2004, 4). He goes on to cite schools' reliance on standardized testing as something that leads to "uniformity among students while neglecting the concept of developing students to their fullest potential." We ignore the arts at our peril.

Our students come to school with a good dose of natural wonder. They have many questions about the world, and they are natural experimenters. A small child can occupy herself for hours with sand, water, and several different size containers. All too often, we destroy this sense of wonder by forcing learning into specific molds and procedures.

> Adult wonder is intricately bound up in a set of skills and habits—formerly known as the liberal arts—that are not specialized but general to all vocations and avocations. These skills . . . are fed by practice far more than by direct instruction; they are nurtured by meaningful and novel work rather than dull repetition. What kills wonder is habituated boredom; what grows it is inspired practice. . . . we are systematically killing wonder even in our best schools. (Roberts 2004, 31)

Roberts goes on to say that "'high stakes accountability' has squeezed wonder out of the classroom." We have too much to do, to prepare for, to allow us to take the time to wonder. Learning can be very superficial without wonder.

Stigler and Hiebert (1999), in their study of mathematics teaching, *The Teaching Gap*, characterize American math classes primarily as learning terms and practicing procedures (41).

Alfie Kohn (2004) laments the loss of joy in our schools during this time of demanding ever higher standards.

> Richer thinking is more likely to occur in an atmosphere of exuberant discovery, in the kind of place where kids plunge into their projects and can't wait to

pick up where they left off yesterday. Numerous studies have demonstrated how interest drives achievement, ongoing interest in a general topic more than transient interest in a specific activity, and excited interest more than the casual, mild kind. (Kohn 2004, 36)

Communication

Finally, everything revolves around communication. We must teach our students to understand and to be understood. Once again, this goes far beyond simple decoding and calculating. In fact, the idea extends to other languages, such as musical notation, computer code, French, mathematical equations, and maps, to name a few.

An expanded concept of language and communication should pervade all that we do with our students. Ideas that cannot be expressed in some intelligible way essentially do not exist. By the same argument, arguments that the receiver does not have the capacity to understand remain hidden.

The constant development of a literate community in the widest sense is vital, once again, to the successful implementation of a democracy. Our society is bombarded with scientific, philosophical, political, and spiritual information. The data come in many forms, such as words, pictures, cartoons, television, video, movies, packaged instructions, the backs of cereal boxes, and on and on.

To operate in our current world is to be multilingual in many ways. Building an argument, explaining why, describing accurately, writing a computer program, understanding the iconography in film and literature, noticing the subtext in propaganda, seeing the meaning of a work of art—these are some of the literacies necessary for a rich life, a life of continuous involvement and learning.

How can we hope for collaboration without communication skills? How can we hope for diplomacy without communication skills? And how can these skills develop without kindness, thinking, communication, and problem solving? In fact, these four pillars of curriculum are in ways inseparable, one from the other.

That is exactly why all four need to be present throughout our educations, and our educations begin at birth and end at death. According to Daniel Goleman in his 1995 book, *Emotional Intelligence*, "The impact of parenting [teaching] on emotional competence starts in the cradle" (192). Our very survival as a species depends on these four foundations of learning and growing.

A LIFETIME OF CONSTRUCTING MEANING

From a constructivist point of view, we all make meaning from our experiences. How are we going to make this meaning and share it with others without the four pillars of curriculum? Vygotsky would argue that language itself is a result of social interaction. You point at the rock and say "grop." Another points at the rock and says "rock." Eventually there has to be some consensus on the name of the object for communication to result.

If we fight over the name, if we fail to think about why we need to find a common word, if we cannot solve this problem, we remain isolated entities unable to share and consequently expand knowledge.

Perhaps this all seems a bit abstract and even dramatic. However, in subsequent chapters, I hope to demonstrate concrete applications of these four pillars of the super-scaffold. An ideal vision is not a bad goal for guiding our real-world practice. Even if we never get there, we at least know where we are going and why it is a good direction.

The goal of this book is to develop an argument for the inclusion of kindness, thinking, problem solving, and communication in every lesson for every child every day. These are the starting points for building curricula, not the atomization of the traditional disciplines.

In a 2004 book by Dennis Littky and Samantha Grabelle, the authors list what they believe are the fourteen goals of education derived from Littky's thirty years of experience. While not a perfect match, each of Littky's goals incorporates one or more or the four pillars developed above. Here are his goals, with K (kindness), T (thinking), PS (problem solving), or C (communication) after each one to mark the correspondence:

Be lifelong learners (T, PS, K)
Be passionate (K, PS)
Be able to take risks (K, PS)
Be able to problem solve and think critically (T, PS, K)
Be able to look at things differently (T, PS, K)
Be able to work independently and with others (K, C)
Be creative (PS, K, T)
Care and want to give back to their community (K)
Persevere (PS, T)
Have integrity and self-respect (K)
Have moral courage (K)
Be able to use the world around them well (K, PS, T, C)
Speak well, write well, read well, and work well with numbers (C, T, PS, K)
Truly enjoy their life and their work (C, T, PS, K) (Littky and Grabelle
    2004, 1)

A 1992 report, Head Start: The Emotional Foundations of School Readiness published by the National Center for Clinical Infant Programs claims that a student's success is based on knowing how to learn, which includes such qualities as confidence, curiosity, intentionality, self-control, relatedness, capacity to communicate, and cooperativeness (Goleman 1995, 193–94). The overlap with our four pillars of curriculum is once again glaringly apparent.

THE SHRIVELING OF AMERICAN EDUCATION

Many schools' curricula are already narrowing, as the main educational goal has shrunk to passing the test, not liberating the human spirit. If penalties result from poor scores on reading, writing, and mathematics tests, then those are the subjects that we teach.

A poor curriculum becomes poorer still with the new lack of time for art, music, literature, extended inquiry, creative expression, trips to the zoo, research, community involvement, good nonfiction essays, and gazing at the stars. Where is the thinking and reflection? Where is the building of decent, kind human beings? Where is the extension of problem solving beyond what is asked in the math textbook? Where is the ability to interact with complex worlds of ideas, expressing one's opinion and understanding the opinions of others in many forms of communication? Is this the promise of education to America's children? I hope not.

To return to Paul Boyer's memoir of his father one more time,

> Instead, the most meaningful education revealed connections—between subjects, between people, and between cultures. "To be truly educated means going beyond the isolated facts, putting learning in a larger context and, above all, it means discovering the connectedness of things," he argued. In his view, art and music were as important as math and science because they were all expressions of human achievement and powerful means of communication. Likewise, service learning was not a distraction from academic study, but an integral part of becoming an engaged citizen. Putting all this, and more, together into a coherent whole was what a good school was all about. (2005, 40)

Now more than ever, the changing world demands that we change the curriculum. Education is a moral act, and part of the ethical imperative of an educator is to provide students with the tools for survival and the chance at the good life. On one level, this means the ability to appreciate the world around us, to understand how to recreate oneself, and how to engage meaningfully with the community. It means the ability to nurture one's own spiritual well-being. Asking students to take an active part in their communities, through either political or social activist activities, helps form habits of caring, involvement, curiosity, and commitment.

2

Kindness: Some Examples

Billy is a marginal student, both academically and socially. When Mrs. Smith asks him to stand in class and answer an open-ended literature question, he is in a no-win situation. First, to answer the question requires some creative risk, since there is no correct answer and the question requires some speculation. If he says nothing or something minimal, then he is seen as a "dumby," belittled with hardly audible scoffs from among his peers.

If he gives an interesting answer, then he is equally at risk of being a "nerd," probably hearing similar groans from others in the class. This is a painfully familiar picture.

Mrs. Smith, and probably the school as a whole, has failed to create a safe environment, without which learning is surely hampered. Bernice Lerner, acting director of the Center for Advancement of Ethics and Character at Boston University's School of Education, sees teaching biography as a means of helping students appreciate and create a safe and secure school. She tells us that

> educators, too, can capitalize on students' natural interest in other people's lives. In fact, in striving to promote good character, teachers ought to put before young people exemplars who have struggled and endured, luminaries whose actions demonstrate the human capacity for nobility, integrity, courage, and compassion. By encountering such individuals, students may learn that they are not alone, that others who have gone before them have found ways of coping, of overcoming hardship, of responding to difficult situations in well-considered, constructive ways. To the extent that we teachers carry a repertoire of stories—about both famous and lesser-known individuals—we have at our disposal a vital means of educating for virtue. (Lerner 2005, 37)

Lerner goes on to develop examples of stories that show how students can be "helped to feel safe and well cared for, to know what it means to treat others and their property with respect, and to earn the esteem that comes from contributing in positive ways to an ordered society" (2005, 37).

I remember a math teacher of my own who referred publicly to incorrect answers, even to difficult problems requiring students to take some real risks, as "garbage." Now, why would I want to take the chance of having my response openly mocked by the instructor? I would not.

This is exactly the problem. How can we expect students to take risks, try out new ideas and thinking, and speculate if they live in a world of fear of mockery? According to Eliot Eisner "the social and emotional life of the child needs to be as much a priority as measured academic achievement— perhaps an even greater priority" (2005, 18).

In fact, the 1992 report Heart Start from the National Center for Clinical Infant Programs makes the point

> that school success is not predicted by a child's fund of facts or precocious abil- ity to read so much as by emotional and social measures: being self-assured and interested; knowing what kind of behavior is expected and how to rein in the impulse to misbehave; being able to wait, to follow directions, and to turn to teachers for help; and expressing needs while getting along with other chil- dren. (Goleman 1995, 193)

Eric Jensen tells us that

> in a classroom, emotional states are an important condition around which ed- ucators must orchestrate learning. Students may be bored with the lesson, afraid of an upcoming test, or despondent about a drive-by shooting. They might be hyper about an upcoming sporting event, the preceding physical ed- ucation class, or a relationship. Instead of trying to eliminate the emotions so we can get to the "serious cognitive" learning, it makes more sense to integrate them into our curriculum. (1998, 94).

A key word of Jensen's is *integrate*. We are not necessarily talking about adding yet more to an already overcrowded curriculum. We are talking about manner, not always matter. Math as well as physical education can be taught with kindness and respect. Students can be taught to listen respect- fully to one another, wait their turn, or assist each other as part of the aca- demic program. "Mary, Jim seems to be stuck, although what he has said so far makes sense. Can you add anything that might help him to solve the problem?"

One more example from my own experience. I was the grade-eight English teacher for a hundred-student team. Students could not be heterogeneously grouped other than in homeroom because of a stratified math program, which controlled the schedule. At the end of the year, the schedule was shifted around to accommodate special final exam periods, so I found myself in a general "review" section with my homeroom students. We could go over any material they wanted, from any of their classes.

However, when it came to math, only the students from the most accelerated sections would ask or answer anything. The others were intimidated, afraid that they would make a mistake or show their inferior level of knowledge in front of their peers. What a terrible way to have to go through school.

Once again, I was reminded of that supervisor who advised me never to ask a question to which I did not know the answer. Where is the learning? The stress and fear of appearing inferior had effectively shut off the natural curiosity and desire to learn with which most of these students had undoubtedly begun their school careers. There are many, many talented and kind teachers. All teachers must model kindness, for the sake of passing on this characteristic to their students and to allow maximum learning opportunities in their classrooms.

KINDNESS VERSUS RESPECT

I prefer the word *kindness* to *respect*. Some people may think we shy away from such a word as *kindness* because it is a soft word, while *respect* sounds so much more sophisticated and serious. However, *respect* can be a cover, a shield behind which we can hide. For instance, I might be asked to listen to you with respect. That means that I make eye contact, I do not interrupt, I do not degrade you or your comments in any way, and in general I listen politely. After you have finished, I can thank you for your comments and walk away, having actually listened to nothing you had to say.

Kindness does not allow this. Kindness implies a personal relationship, a connection, a caring about one person by another. If I am kind to you, I do respect you. I also support you, smile, help you out, and honestly engage you in conversation or relationship. I once heard that the basis of all teaching was relationships, and relationships without kindness are not of much value.

> The most important relationship in schooling is the one that binds teacher and student. When that relationship is grounded in mutual respect, high expectations, engagement, and cultural sensitivity, the student is poised for success. (Moses, Livingston, and Asp 2005, 45)

A world of kindness is a world of safety in which people feel protected. One can take risks here, knowing that mistakes or unusual ideas do not draw derision, but rather interest and curiosity. One would not expect a comment to be met with the description "garbage" or with snickers from the back of the room. A correct answer would not earn one the title of "nerd."

I just observed a class in which students were looking at data they had collected based on the number of seeds in various sizes of gourds. This class combined grades five and six. The students had all kinds of theories about the connections between seed count and gourd weight, and they were not afraid to share them, ask each other questions, or critique each other's ideas. This classroom was a safe environment in which students could practice inquiry skills and the scientific process, both of which require taking risks and chances. They were practicing kindness as they interacted around the objectives of the lesson.

Where does kindness come from, and why can it be so difficult to find? Does being kind mean that you are not tough enough, that you don't have standards? We appear to fear anything that suggests this kind of weakness. Allow me to develop an example from a discipline problem I dealt with in a high school where I was an administrator.

A young woman had the last period of the day free. There was no way she was going to hang around for her study hall. It just wasn't going to happen. The hard-and-fast rule would be to give her an office detention for every day she cut the study hall. This was the response expected from me by most of the faculty. Rules are rules, and my job as an administrator was to make sure that they were followed with appropriate consequences for disobedience.

I couldn't see the logic. She was not going to go to the study hall. Office detentions, if she even bothered to attend them, were not going to change her behavior and would probably lead to the need to suspend her for not attending. This was simply a downward spiral waiting to happen. I could "respect" the rules, or I could find another way, one that involved establishing a relationship with the student and operating on the basis of kindness.

We had a community service requirement for graduation. This was the kind of thing that many students left to the last minute, then fulfilled with a quickly pulled together, expedient plan. I thought this requirement might be a way to solve the problem, and indeed it was. I asked the young lady if she liked to read and if she liked to act out characters. She did.

That was all I needed. I set her up recording books for learning-disabled students when she was supposed to be in study hall. She had fun, she was in school, and she was fulfilling her community service requirement. At the same time, she was practicing kindness for others. Kindness begets kindness. Respect is of vital importance, but without being tempered with kindness, it can be a harsh adherence to a set of principles. In the process, I had earned the respect of that student and her parents.

Arlington, Virginia, uses a technique called Teacher Expectations and Student Achievement (TESA). The training takes months, with teachers observing one another with respect to the fifteen characteristics taught in the program. Teachers work on three of these characteristics each month. A major focus of the program is to teach teachers to treat the best and the neediest students equally.

As one teacher in the program put it, "There's curriculum, there's method, and there's this [TESA]. . . . You can be a great teacher, but if you can't relate to the kids and feel like they can do it, it doesn't matter how well you know your content" (Gewertz 2005, 1, 14). The fifteen skills taught (Gewertz 2005, 14) are as follows:

1. Calling on students equally
2. Offering individual help
3. Waiting for students to respond
4. Delving deeper into the subject matter
5. Asking higher-level questions
6. Affirming, correcting response
7. Giving praise
8. Citing reasons for praise
9. Listening closely
10. Accepting students' feelings
11. Standing close to students
12. Being courteous
13. Taking an interest, complimenting
14. Using touch to build support
15. Managing misbehavior

WE'RE ALL JUST BIG BABIES

Adults' response to infants is all but universal. We coo and say how cute they are; we want to hold them. We respond to their every noise as if we are having a conversation.

We clap and cheer at everything they do. What happens to all that?

Granted, we need to foster independent action and function. However, why does a ten-year-old deserve any less appreciation as a bundle of potential life? Why do we stop the constant encouragement and support? Does treating a person as an increasingly mature individual mean a concomitant decrease in general kindness? Does an individual life become anything less to celebrate because it has gained some maturity?

Does a person have to be cute and cuddly to be of value? Granted, it may no longer be appropriate to tickle a twelve-year-old under the chin, but that twelve-year-old was once someone's baby and probably still is. Every human being can be loved and valued.

I believe that we all want to be cared for, appreciated, loved, supported, and understood. Can that be wrong? In fact, if we treated each other accordingly, wouldn't that have implications for those "bullying prevention" programs I mentioned in the last chapter? Preventing bullying and conflict implies that these things will happen unless we do something. I agree.

One thing we can do, in my opinion, is to retain the care and appreciation we hold for one another as infants all through our lives. We can continue to celebrate each others' accomplishments. We can continue to encourage and support one another throughout our lives together. These behaviors have immense implications for the classroom and for the atmosphere of the school as well, if not for the world in which we live.

This does not mean that we cannot be tough with one another when we need to be. It does not mean failing to teach someone to stand on his own two feet or not to solve problems for oneself. Kids need to develop passion for their beliefs and be ready to defend what they believe is right. However, this can and should all take place in the context of support and caring.

We need to teach our students to care for one another, to be kind to each other at all times. We can hold each other with our voices, attitudes, and gestures as much as with our arms. And the best part is that these habits of emotional intelligence can indeed be taught. There are numerous examples of successful programs that help young and older people to understand social cues, to read facial expressions, and to be more mindful of their own feelings.

Daniel Goleman alone cites the following programs in his 1995 book *Emotional Intelligence*: The Child Development Project, Paths, Seattle Social Development Project, Yale-New Haven Social Competence Promotion Program, Resolving Conflict Creatively Program, and the Improving Social Awareness-Social Problem Solving Project. Just as an example, the evaluation of this last program, involving students in grades K–6, showed the following results comparing participants to nonparticipants (309):

- More sensitive to others' feelings
- Better understanding of the consequences of their behavior
- Increased ability to "size up" interpersonal situations and plan appropriate actions
- Higher self-esteem
- More prosocial behavior
- Sought out by peers for help
- Better handled the transition to middle school
- Less antisocial, self-destructive, and socially disordered behavior, even when followed up into high school
- Improved learning-to-learn skills
- Better self-control, social awareness, and social decision making within and outside the classroom

We could spend a lot more time on those all-important academics if we first established an atmosphere in which we could avoid spending so much time dealing with emotional problems, discipline, and social issues. We need to know our students as unique individuals. A recent book, *Preparing Teachers for a Changing World*, edited by Linda Darling-Hammond and John Bransford, was released at the 57th annual conference of the American Association of Colleges for Teacher Education in 2005. Among its recommendations for teacher training was the following:

> The authors also write that new teachers should be prepared to teach students of different cultural and linguistic backgrounds and be able to connect those diverse learners to the subjects being taught. "For this connection to occur, teachers must know their students—who they are, what they care about, what language they speak, what customs and traditions are valued in their homes," the book says. Opportunities to learn about diversity should not be isolated to a course or two, it adds, but spread throughout the curriculum. (Jacobson 2005a, 10)

CARING IS CARING

Think of the way we respond to a baby's sadness or crying. Our instincts are to hold and comfort. Tolerating the unhappiness of a child is not easy. Should we be any more willing to tolerate the unhappiness of a young adult? Holding another person does not have to be a physical contact. A look or a kind word can be enough. A gesture of support, an offer of assistance, or an offer of empathy may do just as well. And despite all the laws and fears to the contrary, sometimes the best medicine is a good hug. People who are taught not to be afraid of their own and others' feelings can give each other a hug or hold each others' hands with less fear of this immediately becoming the basis for some sort of unwanted touch or harassment.

We can model conflict resolution for infants, and there is no reason to discontinue reinforcing those models as children grow into adulthood.

> Effective social and emotional learning requires diligent attention to explicitly teaching social and emotional skills, but students also need opportunities to see skills modeled, to practice emerging skills, to apply skills in novel situations, and to receive feedback and reinforcement. (Johnson, Poliner, and Bonaiuto 2005, 63)

We are often willing to get angry or frustrated with inanimate objects, yet hopefully we can find it within ourselves to be more patient with little children. We need to model patience in all aspects of our lives.

This is not to say that we can never get angry or impatient. These are real feelings, and we have to learn to deal with them. However, we tend to find more resilience when interacting with small children than we do interacting with them as they grow older and certainly with other adults. What I am suggesting is that we continue to treat one another as the same precious human beings needing love and support as we do infants throughout our lives.

This is not to say that we should not allow children to grow up. They have to learn to deal with the world's frustrations and setbacks, as we all do. There are good days and bad days. There are impatient people, bullies, and disappointments. However, my suggestion is that we continue to model our attitude toward infants with all human beings at all ages.

We should not tolerate anyone's unnecessary suffering. Why should any student feel embarrassed to take a guess at a difficult problem? Why should any student fear her classmates or a sarcastic response from the teacher? Why should any student fear the expression of emotion in himself or others? Conflict may be a necessary part of life. I want to read, but the baby is screaming. However, positive conflict resolution can also be a part of life.

Goleman refers to a program called Self Science. "Students in Self Science learn that the point is not to avoid conflict completely, but to resolve disagreement and resentment before it spirals into an out-and-out fight" (1995, 266).

Rodney King's famous expression, now overworked to the point of being a joke, is "Can't we all just get along?" Perhaps the time has come to end this cliché and make it a basic part of reality. We send and receive mixed messages about being a community. It seems to me that we are asked to celebrate diversity while, at the same time, not draw attention to it.

Once again, we are apparently allowed to point out that one baby is thin while another is chubby; one has curly hair while another is bald. They are all cute. They are all beautiful. When do we cease to be a collection of many different beauties and become a bunch of "isms" instead, such as ageism, sexism, racism, bodyism, and on and on? We can make positive attitudes the underpinning of our classrooms. One basis for every lesson every day can be the creation of a safe, supportive, caring attitude of kindness and respect for every living being in our classrooms. And from this idea to respecting inanimate objects, especially those belonging to others, is not a huge jump.

STRESS

Life is stressful. We have to take care of ourselves, make a living, make friends, and get along in the world. Why on earth would we add to the stress that already exists by being unkind to one another? Enough has been written on the science of stress so that I will not again here elaborate on the brain chemistry of this destructive force. However, a quick review of stress in general is in order.

The evolution of our stress response is substantially behind our social evolution. Its origins are in the "fight-or-flight" response of our primitive ancestors. This was a survival mechanism. We had to size up a situation instantaneously, without contemplation or much rational thought. When we encountered a dangerous, threatening, or opportunistic situation, there was no time for reflection. We could fight, we could run for our lives, or we could mate: all survival mechanisms that could not tolerate hesitation.

The stress reaction would release various hormones into our bodies, which were designed to help. Blood pressure and heart rate would increase. Blood would be diverted from the digestive and immune systems to the large muscle groups. Breathing rate increased. Blood-clotting agents were released into the blood stream. All of this made sense if you were about to fight or run for your life or capture a mate.

However, these were meant to be temporary adjustments, lasting for a short while. Unfortunately, the stress response we experience today is not unlike that of long ago, but now we can find ourselves in lives of long-term, even continuous stress. Worry about bullies, being teased by other students, deadlines, important exams, insecure job status, and domineering supervisors can and do all exert stress on our lives.

Those helpful short-term stress responses can have deleterious, even deadly effects when they go on for too long. A compromised immune system can lead to chronic illness, as a compromised digestive system can lead to worried stomach aches. More serious are the blood-clotting elements, which may be the source for heart attacks. Certain hormones released during the stress response actually break down brain cells in the hippocampus, causing potentially permanent memory issues. Consequently,

> our stress mechanism doesn't differentiate between physical and emotional danger. Since most contemporary stress results from emotional problems, our stress responses are often maladaptive. (Sylwester 1995, 38)

Clearly, a little stress can be a good thing. When students are not challenged, they easily become bored. However, learning quickly becomes impaired when stress levels become too high. We should be teaching in what psychologist Lev Vygotsky calls the student's zone of proximal development, somewhere between what is too easy and what is too challenging (Foote, Vermette, and Battaglia 2001, 22). The lowest level results in boredom, while the highest in stress and fear of failure.

Memory and emotion are inextricably connected, with much less learning taking place when students' minds are diverted by worries and concerns. Even the work itself, if too challenging, can cause students to give up, believing that there is no point in trying to accomplish the impossible.

This brings us back to kindness. A safe and supportive classroom and school must, if not relieve stress, at the very least not add to it. Again, we should be teaching our students how to work and play supportively together. In fact, some teachers could stand to learn the same thing.

Being "tough" in class does not automatically beget better teaching and learning. If tough means only that the demands are high, that students fear failure, and that they drive themselves unduly, I cannot see toughness as ultimately healthy. High standards, on the other hand, with the proper supports, scaffolding, and encouragement, can result in a healthy and challenging educational and life experience.

A point to make here is that education is a part of life. We might even say that it is all of life, with school simply being a special case of the larger situation. The manner in which we treat one another outside and inside the classroom should be seamless. If we believe in treating one another with kindness on the street, in the supermarket, and on line at the movie theater, then I see no difference in the way we should treat people in the school and classroom. All of life is a lesson in getting along. We are fortunate to have the opportunity to reinforce this idea in our classrooms, and we would be negligent not to take advantage of it.

We hear so much about schools preparing our children to take their place in the workforce and as responsible citizens in a democratic society, both worthy goals. A recent copy of the Association for Supervision and Curriculum Development's (ASCD's) *Education Update* had this to say about character education, civic education, social and emotional learning, and service learning:

> Each of these approaches recognizes that a nation dedicated to democratic freedom requires citizens who possess the knowledge, skills, virtues, and commitment necessary for active engagement in public life.
> To be so engaged, students must graduate from school as ethical, responsible, and engaged citizens with strong inter- and intrapersonal skills.

Furthermore, the same issue defines social-emotional learning specifically as

> the process of acquiring the skills to recognize and manage emotions, develop caring and concern for others, establish positive relationships, make responsible decisions, and handle challenging situations effectively. The core instructional approaches include direct instruction and adult modeling.

In fact, the article concludes, as we have been arguing, "that each of the four approaches [character education, civic education, emotional learning, service learning] is connected to the core academic standards. Schools should review existing national, state, and district standards to develop local examples" (ASCD Community 2005, 7).

Once again, we do not have to see teaching our students kindness as yet another add-on to an already overloaded curriculum. Goleman tells us, "Emotional lessons can merge naturally into reading and writing, health, science, social studies, and other standard courses as well." In fact, the Child Development Project, developed in Oakland, California, under the directorship of psychologist Eric Schaps, "offers a prepackaged set of materials that fit into existing courses."

> Thus first graders in their reading class get a story, "Frog and Toad Are Friends," in which Frog, eager to play with his hibernating friend Toad, plays a trick on him to get him up early. The story is used as a platform for a class discussion about friendship, and issues such as how people feel when someone plays a trick on them. (Goleman 1995, 272)

BULLYING AND GETTING ALONG

The world is full of bullies. One has only to study history, current or ancient. We need to be aware of how we act, how we model behavior in front of and with kids from birth right on through their years of formal education. Ample evidence exists that infants begin to develop patterns of behavior, particularly emotional responses like empathy, at extremely early ages.

One study cited by Goleman suggests that "the roots of empathy can be traced to infancy. Virtually from the day they are born infants are upset when they hear another infant crying—a response that some see as the earliest precursor to empathy" (1995, 98). There are numerous examples of successful school programs that help students understand their feelings and those of others. In this way, an integrated part of what we do can be helping our students to become the kind of people we hope them to be. For instance, Goleman refers to the Self Science Program, which has been in use for over twenty years, "as a model for the teaching of emotional intelligence" (268).

We are all familiar with the overt, physical bullying of the playground. But there are other, more insidious forms of harassment, which are very damaging to students and certainly impair their ability to function in school. Think of the constantly forming and reforming alliances among students. Who is "in" and who is "out" is a daily question. The children who make these determinations are as much bullies as any tough guy on the playground.

Here is where techniques like group work, working in teams or pairs, can have a real impact. Putting students in situations where they must rely on one another can help them learn to get along. At the same time, one can help teach the perennial outsider the social skills such as respecting personal space, not interrupting, and reading other social cues that help her reenter the mainstream of student interaction.

One caveat here is that assigning group work alone does not necessarily help build social skills and kindness. Too often, teachers put students in groups, assign tasks, but then forget that they also need to train the kids in the expected behaviors. Children do not necessarily have an innate sense of how to conduct a conversation or debate without resorting to various sorts of antisocial behavior. Group work is a two-step process, or at least a two-track process. Teachers need to instruct their students in how to be a group as well as in the group's ultimate academic tasks.

We must be vigilant in watching for the more subtle forms of cruelty. We need to watch for situations when groups of students turn their backs on another child or when a group laughs at or mocks another. Kids can be very cruel to one another. A simple refusal to allow a child into a playground game can be devastating. How can that student concentrate on schoolwork when his focus is on his peers' rejection? Teaching and learning simply cannot be maximized in an atmosphere of fear, unhappiness, anger, or feelings of isolation.

> Emotion obviously dominates reason in many attentional decisions, and a stressful situation can chemically trigger an intense focus on something unimportant—such as when we work on an unimportant task to avoid facing a looming deadline on an important project. (Sylwester 1995, 80)

Punishing bullies probably just makes them more angry. If anyone needs support, it is likely to be the bully herself. People are not usually mean for no reason. Anger does not arise out of nothing. We need to take the time to understand why people act the way they do, then try to give them the skills to perform in a more socially acceptable manner. Some programs and studies clearly illustrate that we can intervene early and successfully in helping people develop into socially successful members of the group.

In the words of Nell Noddings, Lee and L. Jacks Professor of Education, Emerita, at Stanford University,

> In his 1818 *Report of the Commissioners for the University of Virginia*, for example, Thomas Jefferson included in the "objects of primary education" such qualities as morals, understanding of duties to neighbors and country, knowledge of rights, and intelligence and faithfulness in social relations.

Noddings says further that

> great thinkers have associated happiness with such qualities as a rich intellectual life, rewarding human relationships, love of home and place, sound character, good parenting, spirituality, and a job that one loves. We incorporate this aim into education not only by helping our students understand the components of happiness but also by making classrooms genuinely happy places. (2005b, 10)

KINDNESS IN EVERY CLASS

Thus, I would argue that kindness must be an aspect of every teacher's work. There is no reason why we cannot teach all material at all grade levels in an atmosphere of support and social acceptance. Kindness does not erode standards. In fact, it may make higher standards possible. Simply demanding more can result in stress and worry. Forging the positive relationships necessary for students to respect a teacher and want to do their best are more likely to allow for high performance.

Children who are comfortable, feel supported, know that they can receive help from others—these are children who function in outstanding ways. In addition, teaching empathy, a core characteristic of a safe environment, itself demands a calm environment. Much of empathy is learned through people's mirroring one another, and this mirroring "requires enough calm and receptivity so that the subtle signals of feeling from another person can be received and mimicked by one's own emotional brain" (Goleman 1995, 104).

The University of Virginia studied the results of teachers' behaviors on first-grade student achievement. With direct instruction and ongoing feedback, students of mothers with less than a college degree scored as well as those whose mothers who were more highly educated. Interestingly,

> the same pattern held true for children described by the researchers as "functionally at risk," meaning that they displayed behavioral, social, or academic problems in kindergarten. When those students were assigned to classrooms where teachers were more sensitive, warm, and positive—the second set of teachers' traits examined—the children performed at levels nearly identical to those of children who didn't have a history of problems in kindergarten. (Jacobson 2005b, 3)

Remember the math teacher who responded to incorrect student work with the term "garbage"? What if she had approached the situation differently: "That is an interesting way to solve the problem. Can you explain your reasoning? Does everyone agree that this approach leads to an accurate solution?"

The ensuing conversation could lead to an intelligent discussion of the problem, honoring the student's work while at the same time surfacing errors in logic or calculation. My guess is that that student, and others in the class, would be much more willing to try out solutions to new and challenging problems after a lesson like that than if their work had been summarily rejected as garbage.

Whether or not we explicitly devote a class to emotional literacy may matter far less than *how* we teach in our classrooms. There is perhaps no concept where the quality of the teacher matters so much, since how a teacher handles his class is in itself a model, a de facto lesson in emotional competence—or the lack thereof. When a teacher responds to one student, twenty or thirty others learn a lesson (Goleman 1995, 279).

EMPATHY

Empathy is so important in developing emotionally intelligent and capable human beings that it deserves a closer look. According to Goleman,

> all rapport, the root of caring, stems from emotional attunement, from the ca- pacity for empathy. That capacity—the ability to know how another feels— comes into play in a vast array of life arenas, from sales and management to romance and parenting, to compassion and political action. (2005, 96)

Teachers need to model caring for their students. Bonnie Bernard, senior program associate at the nonprofit WestEd, has studied this phenomenon.

> Fostering resiliency in students requires that teachers shift their "intention," states Bernard. "It's really about our way of being, more so than it is about do- ing anything," she explains. Rather than just tolerating the disruptive or over- looking the reticent students, teachers must be mindful about their interac- tions with all young people. "No matter what's going on in the classroom, we can take a little step back . . . take a deep breath . . . and realize that, here in this moment, 'I can smile, I can make eye contact.' And that is not going to take any more time. It happens instantaneously, in that moment."
>   When Bernard surveyed California standardized test results, schools and teachers that established caring relationships with students, communicated high academic and social expectations, and provided means for them to con- tribute to the school community, produced students who performed better than others on those tests. (Checkley 2005, 8)

Or again, as Daniel Goleman puts it,

> it is not enough to lecture children about values: they need to practice them, which happens as children build the essential emotional and social skills. . . . One reason they are so poor at this basic life skill [avoiding disputes], is that as a society we have not bothered to make sure every child is taught the essen- tials of handling anger or resolving conflicts positively—nor have we bothered to teach empathy, impulse control, or any other fundamentals of emotional competence. (1995, 286)

Goleman also tells us that skills of empathy can be learned, particularly through training in nonverbal communication (97), He also quotes Daniel Stern:

> But there is hope through "reparative relationships": "Relationships throughout life—with friends or relatives, for example, or in psychotherapy—continually re-

shape your working model of relationships. An imbalance at one point can be corrected later; it's an ongoing, lifelong process." (1995, 101)

Feelings are less likely to come through words than they are through "tone of voice, gesture, facial expression" (96–97). "Children . . . were more empathic when the discipline included calling strong attention to the distress their misbehavior caused someone else" (99).

THE NEED FOR TRAINING IN ALL AREAS OF KINDNESS

Goleman sees psychotherapy as an intervention for lessons in emotional intelligence children have missed along the way. He suggests, therefore, that we pay more attention to children's emotional well-being before it is too late, so as to prevent the need for later repair (1995, 228).

> Educators, long disturbed by schoolchildren's lagging scores in math and reading, are realizing there is a different and more alarming deficiency: emotional literacy. And while laudable efforts are being made to raise academic standards, this new and troubling deficiency is not being addressed in the standard school curriculum. (Goleman 1995, 231)

Consequently, a major foundation for academic success is emotional success, and that is the reason schools must begin to turn their attention to this crucial issue of kindness. In addition, an atmosphere of kindness is necessary if we wish to maximize students' thinking, which we will examine in the next chapter.

3

Thinking: Think About It

We use the words *think* and *thinking* in many ways in our culture, so many that it can be difficult to explain what it is to think and to teach thinking. For instance, we can express a tentative feeling by saying, "I think this could be the right answer," or we could be definite and say, "I think we should go to war!"

We admonish people to think before they act, and we often speak harshly to others by asking whether or not they had thought about what they were doing. What does it mean to ask a student to think about his negative behavior? How is that different from asking him to think about how his behavior affected others in the class?

If a student is stuck on a problem or question, we might offer as encouragement the words, "Well, think about it." What exactly does that mean for the child to do? The student could end up repeating the problem over and over in his head, going nowhere in particular with the information. We need to be clear what we mean by thinking as educators largely responsible for helping our students learn to think clearly, productively, and creatively.

For me, thinking always meant the series of images and ideas, often connected and frequently narrated, which seems endlessly to be running through my head. It is that little voice between my ears. It comprises many processes and procedures, more than I can name or understand.

Shouldn't we be teaching our students how to use their minds, to think, to do something with all the information around and within them? If we stuff them with facts and figures in preparation for tests, then we make of them walking encyclopedias. And like encyclopedias, they become vast repositories of information but cannot do much with it. There is nothing wrong with knowing a lot of information, but we need to go further. Thinking involves the manipulation and contemplation of information and ideas with the goal of discovering ever-increasing numbers of connections leading to new and more complex information and ideas.

THINKING AND TEACHING

Allow me a brief example from my own education, which might have been helped by someone instructing me in thinking strategies. I was an English major in college, and I taught secondary English for over twenty years. As such, I frequently used the phrase "literary analysis." As far as I was concerned, that meant that one was supposed to somehow, by examination, by thinking about it, come to an understanding of a work of literature, to explain its meaning. For instance, the standard character analysis would usually be an elaborated list of the various characteristics of a character and how they contributed to his personality.

If someone had explained to me that analysis was the process by which one separated a whole into its component parts, that definition would have given me a frame and guide for the work. I would have understood, not intuitively but deliberately, that I was to break the work apart and examine how it all fit together, how the parts gave meaning to each other and informed the whole.

How much explicit thinking do we teach these days? I am no longer aware of many debating societies or clubs in local high schools. School newspapers, which demanded the writing of editorials and letters to the editor, appear to be fewer and fewer. These were vehicles for teaching students how to build a logical argument, how to connect pieces to show cause and effect, logical consequences, and interrelated systems of events. When was the last time you saw a course, or even part of a course, dedicated to rhetoric, speaking effectively and meaningfully? In the age of information, has thinking taken a back seat to information?

Peter Senge has written an entire book, *The Fifth Discipline* (1990), dedicated to how people do not think thoroughly enough to anticipate how one variable may affect another variable in a system in which everything is somehow connected. Clearly, according to Senge, thinking can be of vital importance to the success of a business.

A recent example of enhancing the teaching of thinking is the Engineering for K–12 program, run by professor of engineering Suresh Nair at the University of Missouri, Columbia. This program, being implemented in the middle grades and underwritten by the National Science Foundation, seeks to teach students how to "think like engineers" (Honawar 2005, 13). In other words, students do not just understand the principles of engineering but are also able to apply them.

THINKING AND THE WORKFORCE

We have already discussed the issue of schools' primary function being thought of as supplying the next generation of workers. While I have argued and will argue against this position as the number one purpose of education, ironically, even as industry laments our poor test scores and lack of skills, it, too, is recognizing that the skill set needed in employees goes beyond content knowledge. A Boston nonprofit group called Jobs for the Future held a conference to discuss the United States's poor showing internationally on tests of mathematics and science. According to *Education Week,*

> a prominent theme was how corporate foundations can leverage the time and money they give to precollegiate educators so that high school students will have the math, science, *problem-solving,* and *reasoning* skills they need after they graduate—skills the conference-goers said *public schools do not sufficiently teach* [emphasis added]. (Borja 2005, 6)

Even more ironic is the list of nine marketable skills proposed by a group of business organizations as part of a work readiness credential. The work is being overseen by the Equipped for the Future Work Readiness Credential, part of the Center for Workforce Preparation of the United States Chamber of Commerce in Washington, DC. The skills are considered soft skills necessary for success in the workplace, and the credential would not replace a diploma but be issued in addition to a diploma. The nine soft skills are as follows (Cavanagh 2005, 19):

1. Speak so that others can easily understand
2. Listen actively
3. Read material with understanding
4. Cooperate with others
5. Resolve conflicts and negotiate
6. Use math to solve problems and communicate
7. Solve problems and make decisions
8. Observe critically
9. Take responsibility for learning

First of all, these are the very things I have been writing about. Second, how can they be skills one would verify *in addition* to the skills represented by a high school diploma? Apparently, we are not testing for such things as clear communication, problem solving, and reading with understanding as part of ensuring that our students are graduating with the necessary skills to be successful members of our workplace or our democracy. What, then, are we looking for in our graduates?

THINKING AND TESTING

Many of the people who see the purpose of education as the production of the nation's workforce also champion the current accountability movement. The result, according to Barbara Klein, John D. McNeil, and Lynn A. Stout is that

> our education system increasingly is focusing not on developing children's *aptitude* for learning—their ability to absorb new information quickly and solve problems creatively—but on their academic *achievements*—their mastery of particular subjects and skills as proven by performance on standardized tests.

They see American children "losing the chance to think, dream, explore, ponder—and play." The irony is that our system is killing off the qualities our children need most to appeal to future employers, who want not just "reading, 'riting, and 'rithmetic,' but innovation, initiative, and flexibility" (2005, 32).

We hear about the need for more engineers, scientists, mathematicians. Certainly, these are professions that can and should contribute a great deal to society and our quality of life. If we need more, then we should determine a strategy to prepare more. These fields demand deep levels of creative thinking.

We hear that the backbone of effective democracy is an informed public. However, I would suggest that information is not enough, rather that knowing how to think, to contemplate, and do something with that information is equally necessary. We do not want citizens who blindly absorb what they are told but ones who critically examine the information they receive. That is why we have political debates.

THINKING AND DEMOCRACY

For example, imagine that there were two people running for a local office, one who wanted to strip the hillsides of their valuable lumber and one who wanted to leave the landscape alone. Candidate one says that we need the jobs that his proposal would create. Candidate two says that the trees are preventing dangerous erosion of the hillside and protecting endangered species of animals.

The voter must be able to think. She has friends who are out of work and suffering. She also knows what potential damage the deforestation may cause environmentally and biologically. She understands the information, but now she must do something with it: examine cause-and-effect relationships; long-range results; short-range gains; and all of the characteristics of each plan, including unanticipated results.

Only when a person can take in information and then analyze it, understand its various characteristics, see its potential effects, compare and contrast it to other information, and otherwise think about it, can we say that we have a citizen ready to take his place as a responsible actor in a democracy.

University of California professor of education Mike Rose reminds us that

> as an ideal, democracy assumes the capacity of the common person to learn, to think independently, to decide thoughtfully. The emergence of this belief marks a key juncture in Western political philosophy, and such belief is central to the way we in the United States, during our best moments, define ourselves as citizens. Our major philosophical and educational thinkers—Jefferson, Horace Mann, and John Dewey—have affirmed this potential among us, our intelligence as a people. . . . We mistake narrowness for rigor, but actually we are not rigorous enough.

Rose refers to this as "a model of mind that befits the democratic imagination" (2005, 41).

THINKING VERSUS PROBLEM SOLVING

I would like to take a minute here to distinguish thinking and problem solving. The two processes are at times almost impossible to separate, but I believe they can and should be examined individually. Thinking generally leads to the answer to a question or a better understanding of an idea. Problem solving is more likely to find a way to implement a solution to an immediate situation or challenge. One can think without solving a problem, but to solve a problem, one must first think.

For example, a class might consider the efficacy and feasibility of nuclear power. The question would be whether or not nuclear energy is a good idea. To answer this question, a student would have to engage in a good deal of thinking, which in the end would lead to an informed decision.

If the question were how to build a safe nuclear power plant, we would then have wandered into the realm of problem solving. After a great deal of thinking about all the factors involved, we would have to implement our thinking in the form of a plan that would solve the problem. One might say that problem solving is the implementation of a solution, which is the result of a spell of thinking. For now, I would like to confine the discussion to thinking itself as much as possible.

THINKING IN THE CLASSROOM

We have been aware of different types of thinking for years. Benjamin Bloom's taxonomy of thinking is at least thirty years old (Trojcak 1971, 151). What is interesting is that when I first encountered the taxonomy in a teaching methods class, it was for learning how to sequence a lesson plan, working from the simpler type of questions to the more challenging, or to make sure that you asked various students questions at developmentally appropriate levels. The taxonomy was for use by teachers, not something to teach students.

Knowledge, comprehension, application, analysis, synthesis, and evaluation—the elements of the taxonomy—are different levels of knowing and thinking. These are the tools of thinking with which we could arm our students as they contemplate new information, especially in this postmodern era of increasing popularity for constructivist approaches, which force students to make meaning out of their observations. We need to make the different ways one can think explicit for our students. It is not enough to ask questions at different levels, but we must also help our students understand how to answer these different levels of questions and when to use them.

One method I have found particularly effective and at the same time fun is modeling thinking aloud.

> When teachers model thinking aloud for students, they go through the thinking step by step as a student would, role-playing just what one would do. This includes being puzzled, making mistakes, self-correcting, and checking themselves along the way. (Sapphier and Gower 1997, 200)

Students can empathize with this concrete example of thinking. Remember, just like teaching anything else, teaching thinking needs modeling. What is happening needs to be made explicit every step of the way until students begin to internalize their thinking options. How often have you asked a question and received a shrug or an "I dunno" for an answer? How often have you watched a student stare at a piece of paper not knowing where or how to begin? Students need a repository of thinking tools from which to choose.

Every day after recess, the kindergarten class lines up outside my door, waiting to enter their classroom. The teacher always has a question for them. It is always a categorizing question. She regularly asks something like, "Will students wearing pants please step aside?" Those students are then allowed in the room. She then asks another question, and another, until every child has entered the classroom. These four- and five-year-olds are practicing categorizing, a thinking skill, which can then be reinforced easily in a science lesson or by comparing characters from a story. There is no lower limit in introducing students to ways of manipulating information.

The idea of modeling something as abstract as thinking may seem odd at first, but it can certainly be done. We have already seen thinking aloud. Classic graphic organizers, such vehicles as the Venn diagram, or a math teacher's working out a problem while continuously explaining what is happening and checking for understanding are all examples of "showing" students how to think.

David Hyerle published *Thinking Maps* in 1995. Page iv outlines the long history of the derivation of the maps, starting in the 1940s. The end results are eight visual tools, which the Innovative Learning Group argues represent the eight basic patterns we use for thinking. These eight processes are "defining in context," "describing qualities," "comparing and contrasting," "classifying," "part-whole," "sequencing," "cause and effect," and "seeing analogies" (1–9). The purpose of the maps is to give students practice in metacognition, helping them to understand how their own thinking works and to harness its energy. According to Hyerle,

> Thinking Maps give all students and teachers a common language for meaningful learning. The consistency *and* flexibility of each of the Thinking Maps promotes student-centered and cooperative learning, concept development, reflective thinking, creativity, clarity of communication, and continuous cognitive development. (1–8)

In my experience, students actually "see" their thinking as they use the maps, and different students approach the same question using different maps, thus allowing for differences in learning styles and approaches. Hyerle offers documentary evidence of improved student academic performance as a result of using Thinking Maps 1–7.

Another powerful means of incorporating thinking into the classroom is the use of analogies. Through analogy and metaphor, students can learn to take what they know and extend it to new knowledge, to the as yet unknown.

For instance, most students have played the game of tug-of-war. The teacher might have them write or discuss some of the occasions they've played it and the fun they've had. They could address anything they noticed, such as the tendency of the larger or stronger kids to win. Such a discussion might then lead to an examination of gravity, illustrating the point that two objects both have gravity but the object with the stronger gravity draws the other toward it. In this way, the teacher helps the students move from a concrete concept to an abstract one.

Analogies are potent strategies for thinking about the abstract and for helping students start with their own, known experiences as a means of thinking about new, more illusive ideas.

WHO DOES THE THINKING?

We are constantly asking students to think, but what response can we expect if we do not teach them how? Here is an example from a contemporary math text book that comes close to the right idea but, in the end, fails to allow the student to practice thinking. At issue is the area of a triangle, a new concept. The chapter starts with an exercise, the instructions to which tell the student exactly what to do, step-by-step, to show that the area of the triangle is one-half the base times the height (Bailey et al. 2006, 550). That approach is certainly better than simply giving the student the formula to memorize.

However, why couldn't we give the student graph paper, scissors, measuring tools, and glue, so with her previous knowledge about the area of a rectangle, asked her to try to think through the question by herself? She would need to know such thinking skills as brainstorming all that she knew about the situation, comparing and contrasting, categorizing, and playing with ideas. In the end, she would not only understand the concept, but she would, in a sense, intellectually own the concept.

James W. Stigler and James Hiebert studied eighth-grade math classrooms in Germany, the United States, and Japan as an extension of the Third International Mathematics and Science Study (TIMSS) in their book *The Teaching Gap* (1999). Here is a preliminary description of math classes in the United States.

> In the United States . . . the [content] level is less advanced and requires much less mathematical reasoning than in the other two countries. Teachers present definitions of terms and demonstrate procedures for solving specific problems. Students are then asked to memorize the definitions and practice the procedures. In the United States, the motto is "learning terms and practicing procedures." (27)

The American students applied formulas, which they were not necessarily expected to understand, simply do. Later, Stigler and Hiebert point out the following from a specific class:

> For example, Mr. Jones showed students the formula for finding the sum of the interior angles of a polygon: sum = 180' × (number of sides − 2). He then asked students to calculate the sums of various polygons. Students were to execute the formula; Mr. Jones controlled the method. The same problem could have been presented in a much different way. The teacher might have asked the students to measure the sums of interior angles of various polygons using a protractor, and then try to find some patterns that would help them compute the sums more quickly. Students could have been given responsibility to work out various solution methods—including, perhaps, a general formula. Then students would have controlled the solution method. (68)

By thinking for students, we deny them the opportunity to practice thinking for themselves. When new and varied situations come along, how can we be sure that they will know how to approach questions and use variations on thinking strategies that worked in the past? In the example of the interior angles of a polygon, notice that the phrase "problem solving" is not used. Students merely have to measure and notice, find any connections, and seek out patterns.

Unlike the authors of many standardized tests and writers of traditional, content-driven curricula, a number of the educational professional organizations have recognized this need for thinking and have included it in their national standards. The National Council of Teachers of Mathematics states: "Instructional programs from pre-kindergarten through grade 12 should enable all students to recognize reasoning and proof as fundamental aspects of mathematics, make and investigate mathematical conjectures, develop and evaluate mathematical arguments and proofs, and select and use various types of reasoning and methods of proof" (2000, 11).

The state of Vermont's Mathematics Portfolio Scoring Guide devotes an entire section out of six areas to "Approach and Reasoning" (Vermont Department of Education and Vermont Institute for Science, Math and Technology 1997, 1).

Even disciplines less traditionally associated with the kinds of thinking we connect with school understand the importance of teaching and practicing thinking strategies for students. The National Standards for Arts Education says,

> Arts education standards can make a difference because, in the end, they speak powerfully to two fundamental issues that pervade all of education—quality and accountability. They help ensure that the study of arts is disciplined and well focused, and that arts instruction has a point of reference for assessing its results. In addressing these issues, the Standards insist on the following: . . . That across the board and as a pedagogical focus, the development of problem solving and higher-order thinking skills necessary for success in life and work is taken seriously. (Consortium of National Arts Education Associations 1994, 9–10)

Paige and Huckabee go so far as to say, "Since the time when humans drew figures on the walls of the caves of Lascaux, the arts have been our means of recording human experience and making meaning in the world. They are a sign of a thoughtful, inventive, and creative citizenry" (2005, 52). Eliot Eisner sees the arts as "critically important in the development of thinking skills" (Bradley 2004, 4).

The National Science Education Standards has this to say about inquiry and thinking:

> Students at all grade levels and in every domain of science should have the opportunity to use scientific inquiry and develop the ability to think and act in ways associated with inquiry, including asking questions, planning and conducting investigations, using appropriate tools and techniques to gather data, thinking critically and logically about relationships between evidence and explanations, constructing and analyzing explanations, and communicating scientific arguments. (National Research Council 1995, 105)

Even the prestigious Advanced Placement courses and tests have come under scrutiny. Bruce Hammond, head of college counseling at Sandia Preparatory School in Albuquerque, tells us, "From Fieldstone School in New York City to Crossroads School in Santa Monica, California, some of the finest schools in the country are discarding AP in favor of a richer, more engaging, more student-centered curriculum" (2005, 32). He summarizes the case against AP neatly with reference to constructivist theories, which point to the richer knowledge students glean from thinking for themselves.

> The case against AP consists of what good teachers know in their bones about education: that students learn best when they immerse themselves in hands-on work, and that the best learning involves genuine discovery rather than the mere ferreting out of information already hidden away in the teacher's brain. Modern research tells us that the human mind does not absorb knowledge so much as construct knowledge. Students who initiate and control their learning process retain far more than those who are passive receivers. (2005, 32)

Our students need to know more than the facts of history, science, math, and art. They need to learn to think like historians, scientists, mathematicians, and artists if they are truly to understand these fields. For instance, Standard 6.6 of the fall 2000 *Vermont Framework of Standards and Learning Opportunities* states, "Students use historical methodology to make interpretations concerning history, change, and continuity" (Vermont Department of Education 2000, 6.2). In other words, they think like historians.

Learning information is only part of education. Students must also know how to use that information to create, discover, and find their way to new and more complex intellectual places.

REFLECTION

When I was in a position to hire teachers, two of the most significant characteristics I looked for in a candidate were that he liked kids and that he was reflective. After the thinking is "done" or the problem "solved," a thoughtful person reflects. This may be the most important part of thinking, where the most learning happens. The thinker asks such questions as, "Could I have done that in a different way?" "What worked well and what did not?" "What would I change next time?" and "Were there any unanticipated consequences? Were they positive or negative?"

We have seen the use of metacognition as a means of understanding our thinking when we choose strategies, but thinking about our thinking should also happen at the end of the process. We need to help students understand the importance of evaluating their thinking, reflecting on the decisions they have made: their efficacy and consequences. During the reflection process, real growth can happen. Now the thinker has material, an experience of thinking, with which to work, something to which to apply new thinking. As Joanne E. Cooper tells us, "It is only through reflection on our actions that we are able to clarify and articulate what we know" (2002, 125).

If we assume that generally there is no absolute, right answer to any problem, then thinking should simply open the door to further thinking. Remember my mentor who advised that a teacher never ask a question to which she did not already know the answer? I cannot remember where, but I read a line many years ago that has stayed with me ever since, and I am probably paraphrasing it now. It went something like this: "Teachers who answer your questions cheat you." In other words, if questions and thinking do not lead to more questions and thinking, then the learning process stops. Thinking without reflection might be seen as a kind of dead end. We make the decision and find the solution, but the exploration into the ideas that gave rise to the need for a decision or solution, and the exploration into the processes used to make the decision or find the solution, end.

Obviously, there is a matter of practicality here. We cannot think about everything forever. But what I am suggesting is that we help students develop the habit of reflection so that their thinking evolves as much as possible, so that they become thinkers all the time. One excellent method for reflection is to have students keep journals in which they look back on their work or thinking. These can be shared from time to time so that students can take advantage of one another's insights while contemplating their work. Cooper also says, "Reflection often includes the creation of narratives about one's experiences, narratives which facilitate meaning-making conversations with the self" (2002, 112).

GIVE THINKING A CHANCE

If we want our students to learn to think, we have to give them the time and space to practice. We have already discussed several examples above, including strategies and modeling, that allow this to happen. As with all curricula, there comes a point where one must balance content and depth. I would argue that the depth gained by learning to think far outweighs any loss of content while doing so. If students are good thinkers, their learning becomes that much more effective and efficient. Learning to think serves them for the rest of their lives and applies to many situations. We must provide our students with the time and space to implement and practice thinking.

Thirty years ago, Mary Budd Rowe found that if a teacher waited three seconds after asking a question, participation and level of response improved significantly. The average teacher waits only half a second after asking a question before cueing, redirecting, or restating. By sacrificing three seconds to silence, thus giving students a chance to think about the question, the teacher can provide the space needed for thinking to occur.

> When teachers were willing to wait the 3 seconds, many students who ordinarily did not answer did so, the answers tended to be in full sentences rather than single words or phrases, the answers were at a higher level of thinking, and students were more likely to start responding to each other and to comment on each other's answers. (Sapphier and Gower 1997, 309)

We could also see this space at work in the last chapter on kindness. If the environment was safe and supportive, patient and respectful, then students were more likely to take the risks that come with trying out new thinking and ideas. In addition, if students waited a few seconds to think about the effect their words or actions might have on others, and how they might make others feel, they might be kinder to one another.

The Vietnamese Buddhist monk Thich Nhat Hanh speaks of "habit energy." Habit energy is the way we automatically react to certain situations or people. Perhaps there is a person who always makes us angry; we become angry at the mere sight of him. Thich Nhat Hanh sees this as habit energy, an automatic response. However, if we can be mindful, paying close attention to what is happening inside us, particularly within our minds, he says we can catch the response before it occurs and gain some control over our reactions. In other words, once again, we need to create a space between ourselves and our surroundings, a space that allows us the time, even just a few seconds, to think.

The importance of space to the thinking process is also mentioned in *The Constructivist Leader* (Lambert et al. 2002), a book whose authors show that this space is necessary for groups of people (in this case, teachers) to think through the characteristics of their inner and outer worlds through conversations with others and within their own minds to make sense of things. Even though the book is about professional adults, I see no reason why some of its insights could not be applied to our students. Buddhists meditate to create quiet, calm space around themselves. Interestingly, Diane P. Zimmerman in *The Constructivist Leader* writes,

> As constrctist leaders, we listen differently. Consequently, we learn to silence our own inner chatter to achieve momentary stillness. With a quiet mind, we can focus deeply on other voices, searching for themes and ideas, finding boundaries and intersections, and seeking out frictions and incongruities. In response to others, we employ our linguistic abilities to restate, inquire, or add to what we hear; we encourage others to listen and converse, building the group understandings as we go. (2002, 89)

Zimmerman talks about the creation of "small holding environments that share the quality of coherence described in dialogue forums" (91). Again, we see that the idea of creating safe environments for the exchange of ideas also creates environments that support open and risky thinking. We simply need to decide that we are going to give our students, and ourselves, the safe space in which to work and think without fear.

OPPORTUNITIES TO THINK

We need to give our students many opportunities to think and to explore their own thinking. There are countless ways to do this. The two critical aspects of this are to provide many chances for thinking and always to examine the thinking. For instance, there could be a question on the board: a brainteaser, a math problem, or something about current events. This would provide the conversation starter. The key is to ask students to justify their answers or responses. How did you come up with that? What steps did you go through? Explain your thinking.

Students should be debating social issues, the quality of works of art, how to set up a fair test for a science experiment. They should be learning to construct logical arguments through writing opinion pieces and delivering classroom presentations. Letters to the editor, critiques, political campaigns, and the uses of propaganda are all fair game for practicing how to think and to evaluate the quality of that thinking. We should be proposing provocative questions to students.

For the youngest, the question might be as simple as "Why do you have to wear a coat today?" For the oldest, it might be "Why do you think Lyndon Johnson supported the Vietnam War?" While the answers to these questions may be important, that the student has the tools to approach them intelligently, and then can reflect on and defend the quality of her thinking, is the real goal.

We cannot allow a generation to grow up knowing how to accept and recognize the information they take in but not knowing how to question, analyze, and evaluate it. What good is a democracy whose citizens simply listen to their leaders but do not reflect on what they say and then ask hard questions? Logic, consequences, cause and effect, analogy—these tools of power strengthen a citizenry and its people. Not to question thoughtfully is to give up one's right as a member of a democratic society. History is filled with too many sad examples of the results when people simply follow blindly.

THINKING AND KINDNESS

We have now examined two of our four curricular pillars, but in a way, we have been having one continuous discussion. The four characteristics we are examining overlap and support one another as well as the general curriculum. For instance, how would thinking take place in an environment without kindness? Remember the child who is fearful of responding or the teacher who calls incorrect answers garbage. Remember the child who is bullied, who is shut out, who is mocked by his peers.

At the same time, an environment of kindness cannot be constructed without thought. We need to model and teach thoughtful behaviors, especially as developed by Daniel Goleman. Students need to learn to think about the emotional consequences of their actions and words. They need to think about the meaning of words like *respect*. They need to think about the unintended consequences of what they do. They need to think about the words they choose to use in conversation. And finally, they need to reflect on the decisions they make while interacting with others.

THE PURPOSE OF THINKING

The imposition of information, formulas, procedures, and ideas from an external source are ultimately of limited value. Unless a student learns to think for herself, then the ultimate result of education is a static body of remembered material. We must teach our students to use their experiences, minds, and ability to think to learn, evaluate, plan, and grow. John Dewey examines this purpose of education in *Experience and Education*.

> Unless a given experience leads out into a field previously unfamiliar, no problems arise, while problems are the stimulus for thinking. That the conditions found in present experience should be used as sources of problems is a characteristic, which differentiates education based upon experience from traditional education. For in the latter, problems were set from outside. Nonetheless, growth depends upon the presence of difficulty to be overcome by the exercise of intelligence. Once more, it is part of the educator's responsibility to see equally to two things: First, that the problem grows out of the conditions of the experience being had in the present, and that it is within the range of the capacity of students; and, secondly, that it is such that it arouses in the learner an active quest for information and for production of new ideas. The new facts and new ideas thus obtained become the ground for further experiences in which new problems are presented. The process is a continuous spiral. (1938, p. 79)

In other words, we must teach our students to use their minds not only in the present but also for the rest of their lives. This helps them become more self-actualized human beings, intelligent participants in our democracy, efficient problem solvers, and generally thoughtful people.

4

Problem Solving:
Of Trains and Troubles

A train leaves Chicago, headed for New York City, traveling at forty-five miles per hour. At the same time, another train leaves New York, headed for Chicago, traveling at seventy-three miles per hour. If the total distance between New York and Chicago is 1,236 miles, how long will it take for the two trains to meet?

Can you feel the knot forming in your stomach? Do you remember the pages of these problems, each one a slight variation of the previous one? Do the odd-numbered problems for homework tonight and the evens tomorrow? This was problem solving in high school. Algebra I, I think.

It wasn't really problem solving, though, because you already knew the formula: $D = R \times T$. With a little thought, you could probably formulate an equation, plug in the variables, and solve the problem. Of course, why you would want to know the answer to this problem is a mystery. Perhaps there might be another way to get at this type of problem that would demand more thinking on the part of students as well as be somewhat relevant to their world.

Let us imagine that you did not know the formula above. The teacher asks you to solve the following problem. You want to meet a friend at a specific time and place. You are both coming from different directions. What are all the variables, or values, you would need to know to figure out when each of you should start out for the chosen destination if you are to arrive at the same time?

How do these variables relate to one another? Using whatever means you like, such as diagrams, scale drawings, guess and check, etc., try to determine an equation that represents this situation. What is the least amount of information you need to solve the problem with your equation? Be prepared to explain and defend your reasoning when you present your solution at the end of the week. You may work alone, in pairs, or in teams of three.

How have we changed the problem-solving situation? First, there is no initial pattern or formula from which to work. Second, the problem at least attempts to represent a real situation that could occur in the student's experience. Third, there is one problem to work on, not a page full. Fourth, students must examine the situation abstractly for themselves, play with the issues, ask themselves questions, and track their thinking for later debate on which methods would be successful and which would not.

Stigler and Hiebert point out several interesting features of mathematical problem solving in this country. First, they find no common definition of what problem solving is in mathematics (1999, 123–24). They describe problem solving in American classes as follows:

> In the United States, content is not totally absent . . . but the level *is* less advanced and requires much less mathematical reasoning than in the other two countries [Germany and Japan]. Teachers present definitions of terms and demonstrate procedures for solving specific problems. Students are then asked to memorize the definitions and practice the procedures. In the United States, the motto is "learning terms and practicing procedures." (27)

They go on to observe that American teachers are quick to intervene at the first indication that a student is having difficulty (31). This again cuts off the students' need to think mathematically and actually solve the problem.

James W. Stigler and James Hiebert summarize an American math lesson in four parts, two of which apply directly to the discussion of problem solving.

> *Demonstrating how to solve problems for the day.* After homework is checked, the teacher introduces new material, or reviews previous material, by presenting a few sample problems and demonstrating how to solve them. Often the teacher engages the students in a step-by-step demonstration by asking short-answer questions along the way.
>
> *Practicing.* Seatwork is assigned, and students are asked to complete problems similar to those for which the solution method was demonstrated. Seatwork usually is done individually, although sometimes students work in small groups to compare answers and help one another. (1999, 80–81)

Consequently, students are not so much solving problems as applying procedures to mathematical situations, which they may or may not fully understand. This throws into question the whole issue of transferability and the ability to solve problems through mathematical thinking.

Jacqueline Brooks and Martin Brooks, in their 1999 book *The Case for the Constructivist Classroom*, further remind us that when posing problems for students to consider and study, it's crucial to avoid isolating the variables for the students, to avoid giving them more information than they need or want, and to avoid simplifying the complexity of the problem too early. Complexity often serves to generate relevance and, therefore, interest. It is oversimplification that students find confusing. (39)

In addition, they tell us that "learning for transfer is an intellectual activity that must be nurtured and modeled institutionally in schools, classrooms, and families" (42).

The train problem with which we began is an example of a task that has little relevance to a student's life, offers only limited challenges to thinking, and does not lead to further engagement in more mathematics—or anything else, for that matter. Such problems can lead to detachment, students' seeing their education as boring and of little consequence. However,

a 2003 review of research in multiple disciplines conducted by the Coalition for Community Schools confirms that students learn best when they are actively involved in understanding and helping solve meaningful problems. This is true across all ability levels and grades. A 2003 National Academy of Sciences report found that schools successfully engage students when they "make the curriculum and instruction relevant to adolescents' experience, cultures, and long-term goals, so that students see some value in the high school curriculum." (McLaughlin and Blank 2004, 34)

Milbrey McLaughlin and Martin Blank continue: "For most young people, learning matters most when it is personal and serves a purpose. When students have an opportunity to use or share what they know, they want to learn more" (35).

Clearly, then, problem solving is a central aspect of students' learning, at the core of developing their interaction with the curriculum, for sure, but with the world in general as well. Since they will be solving problems for the rest of their lives, whether stretching their household budget or fixing an engineering design flaw, we must see to it that our educational system gives our students a firm foundation in problem-solving techniques through allowing them to create and solve many varied problems in all academic disciplines.

PROBLEMS EVERYWHERE

When you ask someone about problem solving in school, he generally jumps directly to the math classroom. However, reflecting on the idea more deeply would lead to the conclusion that problem solving is really an integral part of many aspects of the school day and, for that matter, life in general.

A venture to define workplace readiness skills being coordinated by the Equipped for the Future Work Readiness Credential project has identified nine important marketable workplace skills. What is interesting about the list is that it includes "use math to solve problems and communicate" and "solve problems and make decisions" as two separate points. Later in this chapter, we will examine two other of their suggested skills, "cooperate with others" and "resolve conflicts and negotiate" (Cavanagh 2005, 19).

The *National Science Education Standards* sees science as an active process. "Students establish connections between their current knowledge of science and the scientific knowledge found in many sources; they apply science content to new questions; they engage in problem solving, planning, decision making, and group discussions" (National Research Council 1995, 2).

The *National Standards for Arts Education* insists on, among other things, "that across the board and as a pedagogical focus, the development of problem-solving and higher-order thinking necessary for success in life and work is taken seriously" (Consortium of National Arts Education Associations 1994, 10).

Finally, Standard Seven of *Standards for the English Language Arts* states,

> Students conduct research on issues and interests by generating ideas and questions and by posing problems. They gather, evaluate, and synthesize data from a variety of sources (e.g., print and nonprint texts, artifacts, people) to communicate their discoveries in ways that suit their purpose and audience. (National Council of Teachers of English and International Reading Association 1996, 38)

For these reasons, I would propose that we look at problem solving as one of the four fundamental aspects of curriculum in its own right. Generally, the solution to a problem is the end result of a sequence of thinking. In the last chapter, we discussed thinking skills, and in this chapter, we take a closer look at problem solving and our teaching of it.

To give students more practice in problem solving so as to hone their skills, educators can present many assignments as problems to be solved. I believe that we have, in a way, been doing this as teachers all along. However, we need to make the problem-solving aspect of what we do in classes other than math more explicit to our students. They need to know that when they work out a way to make their art sculpture balance and stand without tipping over, they are actually solving a problem.

As an English teacher, I might ask my students to write the final chapter of a book we have been studying before they read the ending. Though a writing assignment and a literature exercise, why could it not also be construed as a problem-solving situation? The student has to do many of the same things she would have to do to find the solution to a math problem.

For instance, what do we know about the characters? What do we know about how they speak, how they interact, what they believe? What is the situation in the story? What do we know about the themes of the book, the indications of the author's beliefs? What are the elements of the author's style? Given all of this information, what questions of plot or theme remain unresolved before the final chapter?

Here are a few items from a list of problem-solving strategies in math (Frank 2002, 10):

- Identify information that is essential or nonessential for solving a problem
- Choose an appropriate strategy for solving a problem
- Predict outcomes in problem situations
- Use trial and error to solve problems
- Use logic to solve problems
- Determine accuracy and/or reasonableness of solutions

Couldn't these strategies be applied successfully to the writing problem offered above? The student has to think through all the information before him and draw some conclusions. He then must determine a way to present the conclusions—how to put together the chapter. He must be able to justify this solution based on evidence from the rest of the book. The task of ending the story involves applying prior knowledge to construct a logical conclusion, which fits the sequence of information, which precedes it.

By presenting this assignment as a problem, an English teacher can reinforce whatever problem-solving steps students already know from their math classes. This is a natural outgrowth of applied thinking, and as we saw in the last chapter, thinking belongs everywhere. So does problem solving.

It is particularly important to note the requirement for the student to justify her thinking and final solution. This is the step that exposes thinking and problem solving to critique, enabling the student to be ultra-aware of these processes and to improve them in response to others' feedback. When dealing with any of the four basic building blocks of education developed in this book, making their use explicit and developing a kind of meta-knowledge of them is absolutely essential, so that students can fully understand what they are doing, noting strengths and weaknesses along the way.

PROBLEM SOLVING AS A GENERIC SKILL

At the risk of oversimplifying the situation, we solve problems throughout the day, from the smallest issues of putting together an outfit to wear to enormous problems such as what to do about pollution in our town. Just look at all of those toys manufactured for infants that demand they fit shapes together, solve simple puzzles, or find a way to get the ball from point A to point B.

Thinking and problem solving are all but inseparable. Imagine two children building castles at the beach. They each want a moat. One digs a ditch around the castle, fills her bucket with water, and pours it in. The other digs a moat, and then connects it to the edge of the waves with a "canal." They have each thought through how to get water from the sea to their constructions, and they have determined different means to solve their problem.

The fact that they have found different means to their common end illustrates the richness of possibilities available for thinking and problem solving when students are allowed to think for themselves, rather than just applying algorithms or predetermined patterns. According to Eliot Eisner, "the best way to prepare students for the future is to focus on the present in a way that enables students to deal with problems that have more than one correct answer" (2003, 8).

Problem solving is a part of life, from day one until death. It is a survival skill, not just a math skill. Primitive humans had to evolve methods by which they could shield themselves from the weather and other dangers, systems for the production and procurement of food, and ways to develop coherent communities. Without solutions to these problems, we would be a species of isolated members who could survive only in friendly environments. We continue to develop solutions to these same problems to this very day through innovations in food production and distribution, the development of police and armed services for protection, and the creation of government to give our communities shape.

Vermont's Framework of Standards and Learning Opportunities organizes standards into two broad categories, Vital Results, which applies to all curricular areas, and Fields of Knowledge, which describes specific areas such as mathematics or science. Interestingly, despite a section on Mathematical Problem Solving and Reasoning in the Fields of Knowledge, there is also a problem-solving section in the Vital Results part of the document. Standard 2.2 says, "Students use reasoning strategies, knowledge, and common sense to solve complex problems related to all fields of knowledge," and Standard 2.3 says, "Students solve problems of increasing complexity" (Vermont Department of Education 2000, 2.1).

Clearly, the Vermont Department of Education recognizes problem solving as a life skill, not just a math or science skill. This idea is reflected throughout the document in too many places to note here. Thus, we have two aspects of problem solving to consider: to teach it as a generic skill and the methods by which we teach it. We have seen that memorizing formulas and algorithms to then apply to problems is not really problem solving. We have also seen how problem solving weaves its way throughout the work we do in schools and, indeed, throughout life itself. Again according to Dewey,

> unless a given experience leads out into a field previously unfamiliar no problems arise, while problems are the stimulus to thinking. That the conditions found in present experience should be used as sources of problems is a characteristic, which differentiates education based upon experience and traditional education. For in the latter, problems were set from outside. Nonetheless, growth depends upon the presence of difficulty to be overcome by the exercise of intelligence. Once more, it is part of the educator's responsibility to see equally to two things: First, that the problem grows out of the conditions of the experience being had in the present, and that it is within the range of the capacity of the students; and, secondly, that it is such that it arouses in the learner an active quest for information and for production of new ideas. The new facts and new ideas thus obtained become the ground for further experiences in which new problems are presented. The process is a continuous spiral. (1938, 79)

I believe that we can interpret Dewey's words "arouses in the learner an active quest for information and for production of new ideas" as relevance and interest. Brooks and Brooks agree when they write, "Posing problems of emerging relevance and searching for windows into students' thinking form a particular frame of reference about the role of the teacher and about the teaching process" (1999, 44).

Alfred, Lord Tennyson made the point poetically in his dramatic monologue "Ulysses." The Greek hero contemplates the role of experience as endless teacher when he says:

> I am a part of all that I have met;
> Yet all experience is an arch wherethrough
> Gleams that untraveled world whose margin fades
> Forever and forever when I move.
> How dull to pause, to make an end,
> To rust unburnished, not to shine in use!
> (Kennedy 1990, 389).

Problem solving often requires the student to pull together information from several disciplines to think through and solve the situation. For instance, a social problem may involve political issues; logistical issues; various people's perspectives; the availability of resources; competing issues; skills of science, math, and communication; and the like. Problem solving takes time and breadth of thinking. However, we have fragmented the curriculum to the point where making such connections can be very difficult. "The fragmentation of the curriculum and pressures of time have made intellectual inquiry so highly specialized that, by 7th grade, most curriculums are departmentalized and heavily laden with information to be memorized" (Brooks and Brooks 1999, 41).

In a previous chapter, we looked at the result of learning lots of information without practicing how to use it. The outcome was walking encyclopedias, students who could answer many questions but who were not prepared to use that information in their thinking or problem solving. This is of concern to American industry as well as to education and government. A key point made at a 2005 conference organized by Jobs for the Future was that American business must find a way to help finance high schools to give students more training in, among other skills, problem solving and reasoning (Borja 2005, 6).

CURRICULUM EXAMPLES

Of course we can all associate problem solving with math, but big ideas, basic concepts, and themes occur throughout the curriculum. Brooks and Brooks tell us that

> problems structured around "big ideas" provide a context in which students learn component skills, gather information, and build knowledge. Attempts to linearize concept formation quickly stifle the learning process. . . . We are all responsible for our own learning. The teacher's responsibility is to create educational environments that permit students to assume the responsibility that is rightfully and naturally theirs. Teachers do this by encouraging self-initiated inquiry, providing the materials and supplies appropriate for the learning tasks, and sensitively mediating teacher/student and student/student interactions. But, the teacher cannot take sole responsibility for the students' learning. (1999, 49)

Here are some examples of how the ideas of problem solving and giving students the responsibility for learning, either tacitly or explicitly, flow through other subject areas of a typical school curriculum.

Art: Given a choice of materials, specific final dimensions, and any style you choose, produce a work of art that illustrates your feelings about a specific social problem in the world today.
Writing: You have 500 words in which to capture the personality of a character such that the reader, after reading your piece, feels that he could recognize that character.
Wood Tech: Given the final dimensions and budget, build a two-shelf cabinet for books that will hold the most weight and waste the least amount of material.

Science: Given several mixtures, each containing three or more different powders, devise a method for separating the powders one from another.

Social Studies: Given a current world, national, or local problem (hunger, health care, traffic issues), study the situation and devise a solution to eradicate or at least ameliorate the situation.

Physical Education: Given what you know about the opposing team and your own, devise a strategy that will allow your offense to score against the opponent.

These are just a few quick examples of how problem solving might open the way for students to exercise their interests, thinking, and skills while developing this all-important talent.

PROBLEM SOLVING IS BOTH NATURAL AND NECESSARY

As we looked at young children, we were impressed with their lives as inquirers. They live in a constant state of curiosity and learning. For them, inquiry comes from exploring and being interested in the world. Through their active explorations of their world, tensions arise which lead them to ask questions about aspects of the world that puzzle them. They systemically investigate those questions, thereby creating new understandings and new questions and issues. (Short, Schroeder, Laird, Kauffman, Ferguson, and Crawfordet, 1996, 8)

This statement, from *Learning Together Through Inquiry*, reflects the work of Kathy G. Short and Burke and once again confirms our earlier descriptions of children as naturally curious, playful discoverers of knowledge and understanding. As we have seen before, the world starts out as a place of wonder, but too often that wonder can be squelched by our education system. Relevant problem solving is one way to keep that world of wonder alive.

In fact, according to Robert Sylwester,

only a small number of our brain's tens of billions of neurons are directly involved in sensorimotor interactions with the environment, or with the regulation of body processes. Most of our brain's neural networks process the complex interactions that lead to the analysis and solution of problems." (1995, 106)

In other words, the primary function of the brain is to solve problems, so what more natural way to teach to it than to pose problems, allowing its natural purpose to be exercised.

Attention to the cognitive system places teachers in the role of *learning facilitators* and students in the role of *authentic problem solvers and decision makers.* A facilitator sets the stage for learning. A facilitator does *not* tell or profess to know all the answers, but prepares the classroom with problems to be solved and arranges supporting materials for solutions as students address their need to know. (Given 2002, 8)

Robert J. Marzano has spent much time studying and analyzing what works in teaching. One of his recommendations is for teachers to have students engage in complex tasks, thus requiring that they examine material in various and unique ways. His suggestions for complex tasks include "problem solving, decision making, systems analysis, creating metaphors, and creating analogies" (2003, 119).

However, Marzano does not stop here. As we discussed in the chapter on thinking and above, metacognition, making student thinking and problem solving explicit to the student herself, is of utmost importance. "Being involved in such tasks certainly enhances students' understanding of content. However, it is the act of explaining and justifying one's conclusions that facilitates deep conceptual change" (2003, 119). Add to this what Eisner has to say about making good judgments:

The problems that matter most cannot be resolved by formula, algorithm, or rule. They require that most exquisite human capacity that we call judgment. Judgment is not mere preference, but rather the ability to give reasons for the choices that we make. Good judgment requires good reasons. The disposition and critical acumen that make good judgment possible are among the most important abilities that schools can cultivate in students.

To cultivate this quality, the curriculum needs to consist of problems that permit judgment. Such problems require deliberation and yield multiple resolutions. (2003, 8)

San Diego and Boston made the greatest increases in math scores for grades four and eight of any cities in one of the latest rounds of the National Assessment of Educational Progress (NAEP). They attribute much of their success to placing less emphasis on memorizing algorithms and "giving students greater ability to solve a broad variety of math problems and preparing them for more complex mathematics later in school" (Cavanagh 2006, 1). They are teaching their teachers to be open to students' using a greater variety of methods when solving math problems.

An overriding goal is to broaden students' overall problem-solving skills, rather than just encouraging them to memorize formulas. "We want to make sure they learn the meaning behind the mathematics," she [Kris Acquarelli, math director for San Diego] said, "rather than just rules and procedures." (14)

This focus on teaching teachers how to be more accepting of various approaches to solving a single problem is interesting in light of what Tony Wagner, codirector of the Change Leadership Group at Harvard University's graduate school of education, has to say about educating teachers to increase the level of rigor in America's classrooms.

> And if educators were routinely asked in their work to *really* think—to analyze data, assess research, and solve problems together—would students then be more likely to learn these same competencies?
>
> If such a connection exists—and I think it does—then how do we create an education reform strategy that relies less on mindless, mandated compliance and computer scored, test-based accountability and more on the development of educators' collaborative problem-solving and reasoning skills?
>
> The low levels of rigor we observed in Advanced Placement classes raise additional questions. The main trouble with these courses was not poor teaching, but the tests for which students were being prepped . . . tests that require more memorization than thinking. (2006, 28–29)

The standards movement does indeed require that teachers and schools in general use data to make decisions. An issue, of course, is time and the training needed in data analysis techniques. The system appears to be moving in the right direction, but we need more resources to make data-driven decision making a broader reality.

Brooks and Brooks pick up the importance of the relationship between testing and teaching, particularly in relation to students' experiences of authentic learning through solving problems.

> Because testing drives teaching, most teachers will eventually cease much of their teaching and prepare their students for the reality of having to pass a multiple-choice test. . . . Tests, then, particularly multiple-choice tests, are structured to determine whether students know information related to a particular body of knowledge—usually a curriculum guide or syllabus. The focus is outward, not inward, on material, not personal constructions. Therefore, the overarching question asked by the test is "Do you know this material?" Authentic activities (tasks and problems already relevant or of emerging relevance to students) also relate to a particular body of knowledge, but rather than structuring assessment around specific bits of information, they invite students to exhibit what they have internalized and learned through application. The overarching question posed by such activities is "What do you know?" These two overarching questions are quite different. (1999, 96–97)

Perhaps, then, we need to take a closer look at the manner of assessment for accountability, examining both students' fund of knowledge and their ability to use that knowledge. Surely, teachers should and do model both knowing and using information. Teacher accountability is not the problem, but the manner in which it is implemented may very well be.

We continue to bump up against the difference between holding lots of information in one's brain and knowing what to do with it. Thinking and problem solving are the means for taking information and understanding it, not only as discrete pieces, but also as interrelated aspects of the world in which we live.

Once again we can turn to the needs of industry, democracy, and life itself to see readily why it is so important to know what to do with information as well as to know the information itself. In fact, one can learn to find most of the necessary information, rather than having to remember it, making the processes of thinking and problem solving that much more important. The acquisition of information comes from memorizing facts; the understanding of information comes from using facts. A particularly powerful means of using those facts is to solve problems of relevance and complexity.

CONFLICT RESOLUTION AND PROBLEM SOLVING

Earlier, we saw that two workplace skill recommendations were "Cooperate with others" and "Resolve conflicts and negotiate." Both of these recommendations are extensions of problem solving. To cooperate means to find a way to get along with others, and to resolve conflicts is to solve the problems we have with other people. If employers are seeking these skills specifically, then we cannot assume that people naturally develop these coping mechanisms. Thus, they become necessary elements of one's education.

Getting along with others is a basic life survival skill. Certainly, it incorporates the ability to analyze a situation, then make problem-solving decisions to avoid conflict. A key element of many workplace situations is to be able to work cooperatively. Unless an individual can find ways to tolerate others, to be tolerable to others, and to resolve feelings of conflict in a peaceable way, continued employment is in question. If you are teased all the time, you can do nothing, you can become aggressive, or you can seek a solution to the problem.

Once again, we turn to Daniel Goleman's work in *Emotional Intelligence*. Many New York City public schools have used the Resolving Conflict Creatively Program. An examination of the program shows how much problem solving is involved. Some students are trained as mediators. When they work with students in conflict, they

> phrase their statements in ways that make both parties feel that the mediator is impartial. Their tactics include sitting down with those involved and getting them to listen to the other person without interruptions or insults. They have each party calm down and state their position, then have each paraphrase what's been said so it's clear they've really heard. Then they all try to think of

solutions that both sides can live with; the settlements are often in the form of a signed agreement. (1995, 277)

So much of this process echoes the problem solving we have been discussing. The students must explain their thinking while others listen respectfully. In this way, they gather information about what happened, not in the heat of the moment, but through reflection of what they saw and felt. There is no predefined method of solution, so that the participants can explore various means of settling their differences.

This process is real-world social problem solving, and it parallels academic problem solving. The students still have to figure out what they know, what they do not know, what they need, where they want to go; they must think all of this through and then experiment with various solutions until all parties can agree. Would that national governments were better at problem solving to resolve their conflicts than they are; too often the alternative is violence.

One of the student mediators has this to say:

"[The program] changed my way of thinking. I used to think, hey, if somebody picks on me, if somebody does something to me, the only thing was to fight, do something to get back at them. Since I had this program, I've had a more positive way of thinking. If something's done negative to me, I don't try to do the negative thing back—I try to solve the problem." (Goleman 1995, 277)

It is sad to think that we have to teach these social skills in school, but on the other hand, school may present the perfect opportunity to do so. If we are teaching the techniques of problem solving anyway, and if part of the purpose of school is to prepare students to live productive and meaningful lives in our democratic society, then we can take the problem-solving template we use in the academic setting and apply it to the social one. It is just another application of a fundamental life skill.

KINDNESS, THINKING, AND PROBLEM SOLVING

By this time, we are beginning to see that these basic foundation blocks of curriculum do indeed form a solid, integrated base. We know that students are unlikely to take risks or try new ideas in a threatening atmosphere. Since one of the most important factors in thinking is to share one's thinking, to hold it up to the scrutiny of others, a safe environment must be in place for optimal learning.

At the same time, thinking is necessary for problem solving and, again, allowing others to critique one's solution. Defending one's position in debate is an important aspect of the learning. Interestingly, we just saw that problem solving can be a cornerstone of creating a safe environment, by using it to work through conflict and disagreement. We ask students to think about the way they make others feel. We ask students and teachers to be accepting of various approaches to the same problem. Kindness, thinking, and problem solving work together to prepare our students for the world around them and within themselves.

Our democracy needs individuals with these skills. People need to be willing to speak up, to analyze and critique issues, and to resolve problems productively and peacefully. If schools exist to do more than prepare the next generation of workers, then their purpose is to prepare the next generation of humane beings, people ready to care and who have the skills to translate their caring into action.

Eisner tells us that "at first glance, the idea of designing a curriculum that prepares students for the future is unassailable" (2003, 6). We cannot predict the future, but we can probably safely say that to survive in any future, indeed if there is to be a future at all, people will have to live together respectfully, thoughtfully, and creatively. The particular information our students will need to know is the subject of many a debate, but these basic foundation skills are necessary for survival and for the learning of any content. Eisner offers judgment, critical thinking, meaningful literacy, collaboration, and service as the crucial elements of any curriculum (8–9).

A FINAL EXAMPLE

Service learning can provide a good example of our three foundational blocks working together. Service learning obviously addresses kindness through civic responsibility, collaboration, and doing for others. If the project involves a public problem to solve and the thinking that goes with it, then we have a complete example of how, regardless of the content, these first three curricular building blocks can support meaningful learning and experience.

For at least three years, seniors at Perry Meridian High School in Indianapolis, Indiana, have worked on local traffic problems with the Indiana Metropolitan Planning Organization. They study real problems and work on real solutions. One group of students spent time "researching, attending neighborhood meetings, and conducting community surveys." As a result, they proposed a monorail system. "Students drew on their skills in math, budgeting, mapping, and design to create a PowerPoint presentation of their proposal to the transportation officials" (Allen 2003, 52).

This project was not about kindness, thinking, and problem solving, but it could not have come to a successful end without any one of these curricular pillars. Students had to work together respectfully, sharing ideas. They had to work with city officials and then with strangers in their survey activity. Having gathered information, they had to analyze and examine what they had learned, thinking through the issues and being sensitive to others' opinions. Finally, they had to produce a viable, respectable, and defensible solution to the problems they uncovered.

Certainly, they had to use much knowledge and skill from many different academic and social disciplines, but again, all of their work was supported by kindness, thinking, and problem solving. These students are ready to take their place in a democratic community, regardless of the specifics of the future. The best way to prepare our students for the future is not to try to guess what they will have to know but to give them the tools with which to encounter intelligently and responsibly whatever comes along.

Interestingly, their project concluded with a presentation. Without the ability to communicate ideas to others, and to understand the communications of others, a person's ideas would remain solely with the thinker. Social structures would be virtually impossible, and the building of new knowledge based on old knowledge could hardly take place. We will examine this vital concept of communication, the fourth pillar of the curriculum foundation, in the next chapter.

5

Communication:
A Simple Concept . . . ?

I have left communication for last because it seems the most simple of the four foundations of curriculum, but at the same time, it can be an endlessly complex link among all of them. For instance, we all know that communication means to give and receive information. That much is obvious. However,

> communication is the key to success in any profession that requires interaction among people and within an organization. The teacher's job requires clear articulation of expectations, encouragement, and caring, as well as content knowledge. Moreover, the communication of content in teaching is far more than just talking about objectives. Effective communication in teaching requires that a teacher have a clear understanding of the subject matter and of how to share that material with students in a way that they come to own and understand it deeply. Beyond directly teaching content knowledge and skills, effective teachers also must be adept at facilitating students' own search for knowledge. (Stronge 2002, 63)

The above passage could easily be referring to many conversations or acts of communication, not just those between teachers and students. The permutations of types and levels of communication are almost endless.

> Communication is not a bolt-on extra; for most species it is a matter of survival. Most of the constant information exchange that goes on between living things is unconscious: hormones waft from one creature's gland to another's nose carrying messages about territorial rights and sexual receptivity; reflex pricked ears and swiveled eyes give mute warning of approaching danger within herds; a bee's complex dance, dictated by some mysterious genetic imperative, directs the hive to a cache of pollen. (Carter 1998, 136)

I can solve a problem without needing to show kindness. I can think without having to solve a problem. But kindness, thinking, and problem solving all rely upon and are related by communication. Without communication, none of the other aspects of curriculum could exist, or if they did, they would be isolated phenomena. We are social animals, and unless we can communicate our ideas, then we cease to be a community and become a collection of nonconnected entities.

> If each author were completely different from every other human being, and if each reader were totally unique, there could, of course, be no communication. There are many experiences that we all have in common—birth, growth, love, death. We can communicate because of a common core or experience, even though there may be infinite personal variations. . . . Just as the personality and concerns of the reader are largely socially patterned, so the literary work, like language itself, is a social product. (Rosenblatt 1965, 27–28)

Even thought, in a way, is communication with the self. "The development of language gave humans the tool needed to lift themselves up to a higher level of consciousness" (Carter 1998, 137). Imagine if the technology did not exist to allow the physicist Stephen Hawking to share his theories with his colleagues. Theoretical physics would be nowhere as advanced as it is now.

As far as Stephen Covey is concerned, "Communication is the most important skill in life" (1989, 237). Goleman summarizes a 1992 report by the National Center for Clinical Infant Programs, which equates a child's readiness for school to the child's readiness to learn. There are seven components to this readiness, the sixth of which is "the wish and ability to verbally exchange ideas, feelings, and concepts with others. This is related to a sense of trust in others and of pleasure in engaging with others, including adults" (1995, 193–94).

RANGE OF COMMUNICATION

As we look more deeply into the idea of communicating, we can become overwhelmed by the possibilities. Starting with the idea of language, we have the spoken and written word in hundreds of different languages, we have computer code, we have sign language. Then there are mathematical, scientific, and musical notations. Many professions and crafts have specialized vocabularies to communicate their unique processes and equipment. Howard Gardner, who writes about multiple intelligences, links each intelligence to a form of communication.

> An intelligence must also be susceptible to encoding in a symbol system—a culturally contrived system of meaning, which captures and conveys important

forms of information. Language, picturing, and mathematics are but three nearly worldwide symbol systems that are necessary for human survival and productivity. (Gardner and Walters 1993, 16)

This is still only the surface, however. Tone, cadence, and volume are all means of communication. Facial expressions, body position, and gestures give us a wealth of information. Sounds, such as screams or grunts, are messages. How we dress, walk, and behave all send messages.

People also communicate through art, song, and dance. And this is only half of the process. If we cannot understand these communication systems, is there any communication at all or simply a failed attempt at sharing information? As teachers, we must pay very careful attention to the concept and practice of communication, both in giving and receiving messages.

People's emotions are rarely put into words; far more often they are expressed through other cues. The key to intuiting another's feelings is in the ability to read nonverbal channels: tone of voice, gesture, facial expressions, and the like. (Goleman 1995, 96)

Despite the fact that there is only an incidental connection between the ability to read feelings and a person's IQ, children who are skilled at reading feelings nonverbally do better in school than those students who are less skilled in this area, regardless of IQ (Goleman 1995, 97).

I remember studying Chaucer's *Canterbury Tales* in graduate school and discovering something very interesting while reading the descriptions of the various characters in the prologue: everything communicates. For instance, the words we choose, such as saying "be quiet" or "silence" or "sssshhhh," reveal something about us. The clothes we wear reveal something about us. We are sending messages all the time, or as Stephen Covey puts it, "Your character is constantly radiating, communicating" (1989, 238). We need to help students understand this, so that they can send and read these messages correctly.

REPERCUSSIONS OF POOR COMMUNICATION

When my son was little, my wife once told him that it was time to "hit the road." Of course, he immediately walked out of the house and punched the street. Think of the classic comic bit, "Walk this way," when the follower not only follows the guide but also imitates his movements. I used to tell my students that whether or not you used a comma in the sentence "The cat ate my hamster(,) Fred," made a big difference to Fred.

We must be particularly careful with communication when we are not there to answer any questions of interpretation. Different people can read the same text in many ways, because the meaning of the text is actually a combination of the words on the page and what experiences and points of view we bring to them. For instance,

> *textual* theorists focus on how readers draw on and deploy their knowledge of text or genre conventions to respond to specific text features. For example, in responding to a mystery story, a reader applies her knowledge of mystery genre conventions to predict the story outcomes. *Experiential* theorists focus on the nature of readers' engagement or experiences with texts—the ways in which, for example, readers identify with characters, visualize images, relate personal experiences to the text, or construct the world of the text. *Psychological* theorists focus on readers' cognitive or subconscious processes and how those processes vary according to both unique individual personality and developmental level. *Social* theorists focus on the influence of the social context on the reader/text transaction—the ways, for example, that a book club context serves to encourage a lot of open-ended responses. Finally, *cultural* theorists focus on how readers' cultural roles, attitudes, and values, as well as the larger cultural, historical context, shape responses. For example, members of a religious sect are socialized to respond to sacred texts according to the cultural values of that sect. (Beach 1993, 8–9)

No wonder that teaching effective communication, both as communicator and message receiver, is so fraught with potential pitfalls. Our job is to prepare our students to communicate with open minds, always being ready to consider any kind of text from multiple perspectives to ensure as much as possible effective, clear communication.

As teachers, we need to be careful not to fall into the trap of confusing procedural and declarative knowledge in reading. Because a student can decode a page of text does not mean that he necessarily understands the text. "For comprehension, it is not enough merely to master effective reading procedures . . . knowledge in the conventional sense of the word . . . is also essential. Such knowledge derives from wide and deep experience and from extensive reading itself" (Kamil and Walberg 2005, 40). We cannot give students too many experiences, and we cannot give them too many opportunities to practice reading and other forms of communication.

How many times have you worked very hard to make sure that your test questions were clear and explicit, only to have some student come up with a perfectly defensible interpretation of what you were asking that had nothing to do with what you wanted? A teacher I work with told me an interesting story of miscommunication. When her fourth- and fifth-grade students asked her if they had written enough, she would often say that their work was adequate. She wondered why their writing did not seem to improve, until she found out that the kids thought *adequate* meant "good," not "a sufficient amount."

Miscommunications can result in laughter, or they can result in tragedy. We are communicating all the time, so we must always be conscious of what we are saying, how we are saying it, and all the other nonverbal information we are revealing. In fact, 80 percent to 90 percent of the messages we give others are nonverbal (Porter 1997). Students need to be aware of the nonverbal aspect of communication both as givers and receivers of information.

Unfortunately, much information is often transmitted and received unconsciously. I read of a teacher who was scolding a student who was of a different ethnicity from the teacher. The adult kept insisting that the student look her in the eye while she spoke, not knowing that in the child's culture, to do so would have been disrespectful. The child sent a message of respect, but the teacher received just the opposite. We must learn to think before we react, to ask clarifying questions, to withhold judgment, and generally to be very careful about our communication.

Yet another price we pay for poorly preparing our students in communication skills is the dropout rate. In several major studies of dropouts, 70 percent to 80 percent cited the need for better teachers and more interesting classes as the reasons they left school, not grades or their inability to do the work. However, the president of the Washington-based Alliance for Excellent Education, Bob Wise, suggests that "the complaints about boring classes mask the real issue: the need for work on teenagers' reading comprehension" (Gewertz 2006, 14).

Researcher Robert Belfanz of Johns Hopkins University adds that students' reports of boredom could very well be a way to save face by not admitting their lack of skills. He adds, "What they are really saying is they're not engaged" (Gewertz 2006, 14). Certainly, students who cannot communicate effectively have difficulty engaging with the material and with their peers, making school a lonely road not leading to anywhere in particular.

COMMUNICATION AND THE STANDARDS MOVEMENT

The standards movement has recognized the importance of communication. An entire section of *Vermont's Framework of Standards and Learning Opportunities* (2000) is devoted to Communications as a Vital Result, meaning that it crosses all subject areas. Also, the standards go beyond reading, writing, listening, and speaking. They also include Clarification and Restatement, Critique, Artistic Dimensions, Notation and Representation (mathematical, scientific, and technological notation), Information Technology, Research, Graphs, Charts, Other Visual Models, Poetry, and Nonverbal Skills.

We can no longer ignore the many forms of communication in favor of reading, writing, speaking, and listening only. We must, of course, include those skills but also go beyond them. For instance, Foster reminds us that

"This neglect should not occur in film literacy courses because students cannot become visual literates if they are language illiterates. One cannot analyze and understand film, or communicate about it, or control its influence, without knowing how to read and write" (1979, 32). The various forms of communication are interrelated and interconnected.

In addition, as we have seen in previous chapters, we are asking students to explain their reasoning rather than just give an answer to a math or science problem. The student must be able to explain and defend what she did in response to the question. To be able to communicate one's ideas presumes that one has an understanding of the underlying processes that gave rise to those ideas. It also opens the ideas to critique and improvement by others, so that the cycle of communication can thus expand the original ideas to greater depths of knowledge and understanding.

NURTURING COMMUNICATION SKILLS

If we are unable to communicate our ideas clearly, then we will fail to deliver our message, and what may be a superior idea will wilt on the vine. By the same token, we must be ready to ask clarifying questions to ensure that we indeed understand what is being offered. This brings us back to the core of a democratic society.

People cannot be content to listen to leaders speak in generalities or to give answers that avoid the question. We need to be able to listen carefully until we fully understand the message through asking questions, seeking examples, challenging what has been said, and generally seeking full comprehension. By the same token, those in government need to stop avoiding direct answers to questions, relying on sound bites, and playing on emotions. A well-educated electorate, prepared to be part of a democracy, would not allow leaders to communicate this way. Holding schools responsible for holding students responsible, in this sense, is vital.

We nurture this ability in our students by constantly engaging them in conversation about their work, their thinking, and their feelings, as described in the previous chapters of this book. In The Courage to Teach, Parker J. Palmer warns that we must not separate teaching from learning, or we run the risk of "teachers who talk but do not listen and students who listen but do not talk" (1998, 66).

We draw students' attention to their words. We ask them to put their thoughts in other ways. We ask clarifying questions. We ask them to represent their thinking in nonverbal, perhaps pictorial or graphic, forms. We ask students then to critique each other's work, to develop the habits of questioning and clarifying. Some of the characteristics of a teaching space recommended by Palmer are that

the space should invite the voice of the individual and the voice of the group.
    The space should honor the "little" stories of the students and the "big" sto-
ries of the disciplines and tradition.
    The space should welcome both silence and speech. (1998, 74)

I once taught a student who illustrated a clear understanding of communication as a means of conveying information or thinking. He was an exchange student from Japan, and his English was not very good. He did not
have sufficient English to answer the questions on a quiz, but he found a
way to let me know that he understood both the question and the appropriate answer. He drew pictures. Japanese is a pictographic and ideographic
language. This student drew strings of little pictures that represented sequences of thought and answered the question.
    We must be careful not to assume that a student does not know the answer
if unable to communicate by conventional means. The challenge is to provide
students with the tools, as many as possible, to make communication viable.
A blank sheet of paper would have earned my student no credit, but his il-
lustrations revealed his competence. Teaching communication skills is to lib-
erate someone's mind and make living as a social being possible.
    We must also ask our students to grapple with complex prose writing. Will
Fitzhugh, founder and president of *The Concord Review* (a journal of academic writing by high school students) and the National Writing Board,
laments the lack of significant nonfiction reading and writing in our schools'
curricula.

> If we don't ask our students to read nonfiction and to write academic research
> papers before they leave school, we not only dumb down their opportunities,
> but also deprive our society of the kind of clear, thoughtful writing it needs to
> maintain a democracy, power an economy, and enhance the daily lives of its cit-
> izens. And we could also find that the decline in the reading of fiction, recorded
> in a recent National Endowment of Arts study, would be echoed in future find-
> ings from the National Endowment for the Humanities. (2004, 35)

If indeed accurate, Fitzhugh's prediction about the future findings of the
National Endowment for the Humanities is frightening. Sandra Stotsky
summarizes some of the report's content: "We do have evidence from a report released in June of this year by the National Endowment for the Arts
of a massive and accelerating decline in adult literary reading in this country in the past twenty years, with the steepest decline in the youngest age
group (18–24)" (2004, 30).
    The National Commission on Writing for America's Families, Schools,
and Colleges reports that American corporations are investing around $3
billion each year to improve employees' writing skills. The report claims
that "while advances in technology have fueled perceptions that writing

skills are not essential, the skill is perhaps more important than ever" (Manzo 2004, 11).

SUBTLETIES

One sentence can have many meanings, depending on its delivery. Thinking back to kindness, we can imagine that what might be a supportive comment could be devastating if delivered with sarcasm or a nasty facial expression. Parker Palmer reminds us that "every good teacher knows how easy it is to respond with the right words, but dismissive nonverbal judgments—and how quickly this will freeze the discussion" (1998, 134).

We must teach our students to disagree or critique each other's ideas with kindness, or at least a kind of academic neutrality, which does not judge but simply responds. Students should learn about cadence, tone, and volume in language, each of which can carry its own message along with the words. In fact, far more of the message is in the delivery than in the words themselves.

Civilized debate can be challenging and rigorous without being demeaning or hurtful. And then there are all those figures of speech: metaphors, similes, personifications, hyperboles, analogies, etc. We use these regularly in our communication without even realizing that we do. What is the meaning of "an angry sky" to a student who understands language only concretely? Why did my son punch the street?

Language is filled with idiomatic expressions, regionalisms, and numerous cultural references. One of Eric D. Hirsch's arguments for cultural literacy is that a common set of reference points allows us to speak in a kind of shorthand, referring to common lines from literature, for instance, to communicate complex information quickly and efficiently. One might suggest action or inaction on a particular issue to a politician with the line "There is a tide in the affairs of men," but if that reference is unknown to the listener, the meaning is lost. (Hirsch, E. D. 1987, 9)

The problem, of course, is our newly global community no longer has a stable, defined set of cultural reference points. We are doing business all over the world, and we must learn to suspend judgment of another's meaning until we have clarified that meaning through questions and reflection. In the United States, we automatically ask each other "How are you?" In China, this question is reserved for close friends or people who have actually been suffering in some way. The possibility of misunderstanding or even insult is increased many times when communication crosses cultural boundaries.

The teaching of foreign languages is crucial, because we communicate our culture through our language. International business and diplomatic relationships demand that we give more attention to the languages spoken by the largest segments of the world's population. In chapter 1, I mentioned a school that chose to add Italian to its curriculum, while logic dictates that Chinese or Arabic might have been a more prudent choice.

THE SOURCE OF CONNECTION

Communication allows us to connect with one another, sharing thoughts, dreams, feelings, ideas, and needs. Communication is the skill that makes all other skills possible, that allows them to thrive and be of use within an interconnected group of human beings. In fact, we create different modes of communication for different kinds of information.

Mathematics and music are entire language systems unto themselves, used to communicate feelings or logical systems that might be almost impossible to demonstrate in any other way. The plastic arts, such as painting and sculpture, provide a means for the artist to express his deepest feelings or visions. There are various forms of sign language for the deaf, an extension and refinement of the gestures that we use generally in our communication. We reconfigure everyday language into poetry. Directors use film to show us stories or to persuade us to buy a product or vote for a candidate.

> Young people need help. In addition to the skills of reading and writing, they need the basic skills of knowledge necessary to deal intelligently with the constant barrage of film imagery they encounter daily in their lives. They must develop a critical response to the media and a knowledge of how the characteristics of film contribute to its ability to influence them, whether in advertisements, news reporting, documentaries, or feature films. They need to develop the means to protect themselves from the more manipulative aspects of film-portrayed violence, which, though not often imitated, nevertheless has its effects. . . . They [teachers] must recognize that film and television constitute, in effect, a visual language which make these media such a powerful force. (Foster 1979, vii)

Graphs, charts, and maps help us not only to understand information but also to know literally where we are. Traffic signals and pictorial signs allow the free and safe movement of millions of vehicles and pedestrians to take place every day. Entire languages are invented to instruct computers on what to do and how to do it. We need to appreciate communication in its many forms and use it precisely. One wrong note stands out in a musical composition. A misplaced punctuation mark can throw off an entire computer program. A poorly chosen word can hurt someone's feelings or completely misrepresent what the speaker is trying to say.

I once worked for a supervisor who used the word *duplicity* when he meant that something had a double meaning. His intent was not to insult anyone, but his failure to understand the actual meaning of the word could have caused some very embarrassing miscommunication. What I am trying to say here is that we cannot teach enough respect for language and communication. It is what allows us to be human beings. It allows us to write history, to record our experiences, to share our innermost thoughts and ideas, and to grow intellectually and spiritually.

THE OTHER SIDE

Poor communication can have all the opposite effects of good communication. It can divide us, cause ill will, create schisms, and generally render situations dysfunctional. Much is written on group dynamics, the roles people play in discussion, and the skills a good discussion leader must employ to facilitate a productive exchange of ideas.

Think of some of those endless faculty or business department meetings where a great deal of talk transpires but very little true exchange of ideas. One of our tasks in helping students learn to communicate is to help them understand the importance of listening to others, not just waiting for their turn to say what is on their minds. Peter Covey tells us, in fact, that listening is even more important than conveying our own ideas when he says that we should "seek first to understand, then to be understood" (1989, 235). He goes on to say,

> You've spent years learning how to read and write, years learning how to speak. But what about listening? What training or education have you had that enables you to listen so that you really understand another human being from the individual's own frame of reference? (237–38)

The Constructivist Leader by Lambert et al. looks deeply at the process of discussion and the ways in which it can go wrong. If you ask a group of faculty members what to do about a school problem, you invite them to take positions before actually examining the situation (2002, 106–7). Allow me to explain.

Let's say you start the faculty meeting with the question, "Should we allow our students to wear hats in school?" Immediately hands go up, and people answer the question with their positions on the subject. From that point, comments come in the form of advocacy, why one position (usually the one held by the speaker) is the most appropriate. Once a person has taken sides in an argument, discussion for all intents and purposes ceases, replaced by defending positions.

On the other hand, if the opening question is something like "Why do you think kids like to wear their hats in the school building?" the facilitator invites the group to explore the situation rather than jump immediately to positions that they then will defend. The authors call this "constructivist conversation," because it creates a space between the speakers in which ideas can freely circulate, combining, recombining, and informing each other, as the group develops its understanding of the situation at continuously deeper levels.

Just as the theory of constructivism posits that we must constantly reform our explanatory theories about reality as we take in new information, this kind of conversation allows the group to examine a situation from many points of view, making more sense of it than if each individual took a stand right off and simply warded off other possibilities in defense of his own ideas.

We can help our students to develop this kind of inquiry-based conversation by carefully constructing the questions we ask and the route we allow the conversation to take. We should make these aspects of conversation and debate explicit until students internalize them. As ever, our task is to model the behaviors we wish students to grasp. In this way, our students practice careful listening, asking clarifying questions, considering several points of view, and not simply jumping to final positions.

This is the art of conversation, of diplomacy, and of community. How can we possibly expect students to work in teams, to develop mutual respect, to expand their thinking, and not to rush to judgment if we do not teach them how to discuss complex issues in this way? Good communication is the glue of humanity and human progress on so many levels. Louise Rosenblatt clearly delineates the role of the teacher in this process in her book *Literature as Exploration*.

A situation conducive to free exchange of ideas by no means represents a passive or negative attitude on the part of the teacher. To create an atmosphere of self-confident interchange he must be ready to draw out the more timid students and to keep the more aggressive from monopolizing the conversation. He must be on the alert to show pleased interest in comments that have possibilities and to help the students clarify or elaborate their ideas. . . . One of the most valuable things the students will acquire from this is the ability to listen with understanding to what others have to say and to respond in relevant terms. (1965, 71)

OPPORTUNITIES TO PRACTICE

For all of the reasons stated above, we as educators need to expose our students to as much and as many kinds of language as possible, every day. Students need to be aware of the languages around them, what they are used for, and how they themselves can use them. To accomplish this, we should consider how to provide activities through which students can practice these various means of communication, both as givers and receivers of messages.

Remember that listening is as important as speaking, understanding as important as transmitting. Parker Palmer tells us,

> Rather than use that space [the teaching space] to tell my students everything practitioners know about the subject—information they will neither retain nor know how to use—I need to bring them into the circle of practice in that field, into its version of the community of truth. To do so, I can present small but critical samples of the data of the field to help students understand how a practitioner in this field generates data, checks and corrects data, thinks about data, uses and applies data, and shares data with others. (1998, 122)

Almost everything we do in school, and later in life, is language based. Cynthia B Schmeiser, vice president for research and development at ACT, Inc., calls reading "the critical core skill underlying all the curriculum areas" (Manzo 2006, 1). Rafael Heller, a senior policy associate at the Alliance for Excellent Education, responded to ACT's study "Reading Between the Lines: What the ACT Reveals About College Readiness in Reading" by claiming that success in science and math is inseparable from success in reading and writing. The study showed that students who met college-level readiness benchmarks in reading were more likely to reach the benchmarks in English, mathematics, and science as well (16).

Those with the greatest facility in manipulating language, whether verbal, symbolic, or emotional, clearly have the advantage. "The importance of language skills in a literate society can hardly be exaggerated. People are judged on how they speak and nearly all academic teaching is done by means of language" (Carter 1998, 154).

Being able to get your way merely because you are more linguistically adept than your opponent is a disturbing concept. By doing our best to put everyone on as strong a communication base as possible, we help our students enter into the great conversations of life with the tools necessary to give and seek understanding and, thus, the tools to make decisions that are sound, not just for themselves but for humanity at large. Communication is a powerful tool, and like all such tools, it can be used wisely and productively or selfishly and narrowly.

HUMAN RELATIONS

We discussed emotional intelligence at some length in chapter 2 on kindness. Here again, what we are really looking at is the way people communicate their needs and feelings. "One key to social competence is how well or poorly people express their own feelings," according to Goleman (1995,

113). What we say to each other, the way we look at each other, the gestures we use with one another, and the manner in which we deliver our messages or ignore those trying to communicate with us all affect the intricate and delicate web of relationships that either holds us together or breaks us apart as community.

We can embrace one another, hold each other, with the way we communicate, or we can be cruel, insensitive, and divisive. I would argue that if we are to survive on this planet, we have a moral obligation to help young people understand the power of communication in all its forms and lead them to use this power to foster productive, peaceful relations among the peoples of the world. Soften the ego and listen to others.

Especially as young children, we receive "countless lessons . . . in interaction synchrony and the unspoken rules of social harmony" (Goleman 1995, 121). As teachers, we must take part in modeling and nurturing these subtle but crucial communication skills. Understanding begins with communication, and communication begins with a sensitivity to the needs of others. A sad example of failure to communicate can be seen in the results of autism.

> Autism is strongly heritable and one of the genes that is suspected to be involved lies in a chromosome that is also thought to harbour a gene strongly implicated in the development of language. This makes sense: more than anything, autism is a defect of communication—an inability to share feelings, beliefs, and knowledge with other people. (Carter 1998, 141)

We know that a strong relationship exists between reading and social skills. "Reading skills and social development in young children are so closely connected that problems in one of those areas can lead to problems in the other, according to two studies published in the January-February issue of *Child Development*." One study found that "children who had a lot of friends in 1st grade were likely to display strong reading skills in 3rd grade."

> "Children do not develop in particular domains independently of other domains," [researcher Sarah Miles] writes. "To the contrary, social development and academic development are inextricably connected." (Jacobson 2006, 8)

Another study found that reading problems and behavior problems caused each other in boys (Jacobson 2006, 8). Clearly, teaching communication, in this case reading ability in particular, is vital to the well-being of our children and to their positive social interactions.

COMMUNICATION AND THE OTHER THREE PILLARS

By now, I hope that the reader has realized that the four pillars of the curriculum are, at some level, inseparable. "To be in the truth, we must know how to observe and reflect and speak and listen, with passion and with discipline, in the circle gathered around a given subject" (Palmer 1998, 104). The productive member of society and, more important, the active member of a functioning democracy needs them all. What binds the pillars together, what makes us human, is our extraordinarily developed ability to communicate.

The word *communicate* itself shares roots with *community*, *commune*, and *communion*. If the other three characteristics are spokes, then communication is the hub around which they revolve and through which they, and consequently human beings, are connected. How can we show kindness and respect for each other without communication? How can we share our thoughts, or indeed record our thoughts for later reflection, without the means to communicate? How can we collectively discuss, debate, and solve the world's problems without being able to communicate with one another?

In fact, according to an article in *Education Week*, more and more states are embracing international education with "attention to the global economy and helping students compete internationally. The same article goes on, however, to lament the narrowing of the curriculum under the No Child Left Behind Act.

> But the current wave of school improvement efforts has led to a narrowing of the curriculum. . . . As a result of state testing programs and accountability measures under the No Child Left Behind Act . . . schools are reluctant to add curricular content beyond reading, mathematics, and science. (Manzo 2005, 13)

Kindness, thinking, and complex problem solving—bound together with communication—make us human and allow us to combine our efforts. The dream of a peaceful, democratic society, worldwide, indeed remains no more than a dream without these skills.

> The teacher's effective characteristics are often a primary concern to the students. Therefore, the teacher must constantly communicate a climate of support and encouragement to ensure that students are engaged in the two-way teaching and learning process. Furthermore, effective management and student learning are clearly related to communication of expectations. Ultimately, being an effective communicator is about repackaging and delivering a message so that someone can receive, respond, adapt, and use the information successfully. (Stronge 2002, 63)

Rosenblatt underscores how the teacher can create a situation in which students learn the habit of reflection.

> Furthermore, the teaching situation in which a group of students and a teacher exchange views and stimulate one another toward clearer understanding can contribute greatly to the growth of such habits of reflection. (1965, 228)

For the next chapter, I have asked four working teachers to demonstrate how they teach our four themes through their lessons. The pillars are not the themes of the lessons, but they are present as the underpinning of class-room activity. Each of the four teachers illustrates how at least one of the pillars can be integrated or embedded into instruction.

I have purposely chosen teachers from different grade levels, and I have asked them to demonstrate embedding foundational concepts that might not be typically associated with their subject areas. For instance, I have not asked an English teacher to show how she teaches communication. I want the reader to see, through real-life examples, that the four pillars of curricu-lum do, indeed, fit throughout the curriculum, not as add-ons but as inti-mately connected foundations for learning.

6

Words into Actions: Implementation

We have argued that kindness, thinking, problem solving, and communication belong in every classroom every day at every age. These four foundations of curriculum are also the foundations of a successful democracy. Discussing these themes is one thing, but actually making them happen is another. To illustrate that the four pillars of curriculum can be part of our teaching and not add-ons, four teachers consented to explain how they embed at least one of these foundations into classroom activity. These four individuals are currently involved with education, either public or private. All four work with students in K–12 systems. Their words are more powerful than any argument that I can muster to convince you that what I have described is doable.

KINDNESS: BELLE COLES, HIGH SCHOOL BIOLOGY TEACHER

Merribelle Coles has taught science for over thirty years, the majority at Brattleboro Union High School in Vermont. She received her BA with a major in education and a minor in learning disabilities from the University Without Walls program of Loretto Heights College in Denver, Colorado. She traveled east to Buffalo, New York, where she continued with graduate studies in biology and chemistry and received her MS in science education from Canisius College.

While at Brattleboro Union High School, she was recognized for her "user-friendly" approach to science. Her classes are lively, energetic, and welcoming, using many modalities of instruction. She is a strong advocate of constructivist teaching practices.

In 2005, she was awarded a Fulbright and traveled to Chennai, India, to teach chemistry at Vidya Mandir School (meaning "Temple of Education"), a private secondary school. The experience was profound and has influenced her both personally and professionally.

She has recently retired from Brattleboro Union High School to pursue her interests and travel. She is currently involved in several freelance curriculum projects and looking forward to what will come next.

What follows is Belle's approach to teaching kindness.

Belle Coles on Teaching Kindness

When I first went into teaching many years ago, I can remember my excitement. I had trained in the sciences for years, and now I was going to have a chance to pass this knowledge on. At times I was worried that I actually hadn't studied enough, that my understanding of all the sciences—biology, chemistry, and physics—wasn't thorough enough. I would envision my classes, filled with interested, motivated students, eager to gain the knowledge that I would pass on to them.

As my first year progressed and I was stumbling and frustrated as all new teachers are, I had a profound realization, one that changed forever how I taught. I realized in a moment of lucid clarity that I was teaching human beings, not science. What I mean by this is that in high school, our primary objective is to teach human beings, specifically adolescent human beings. Science becomes the medium through which we mold these young people's minds. Adolescence is a tumultuous time for everyone. Bodies are changing, psychologically as well as physically. Concepts of self are also forming, and minds are developing higher powers of reasoning. The confluence of all these changes will surely have a huge influence as a student moves into adulthood.

Please understand. I think science is very important to teach and to learn. An informed citizen is essential in today's world. Whether considering workforce, politics, or personal decision making, it is imperative that students acquire certain science skills and knowledge. Too often, teachers of single subjects in upper-level grades forget what elementary teachers know and implement every day. Whatever subject we teach, we teach through the soul of the whole child. Whether or not an individual comes away from high school with a positive outlook on science has more to do with how we teach rather than what we teach.

"Kindness Spoken Here." I have been seeing a lot of these signs recently on my classroom visits. How strange—or maybe not. Kindness to me has always been one of those things that we learn in kindergarten: to treat others as we would like to have them treat us. And yet, in today's competitive world, it is something that we need to remind each other of. In my experience as a science teacher, the longer I have been in the classroom, the more convinced I am that kindness is one element of education that is so very important to the learning environment yet is so easily overlooked and forgotten.

We see this not only in schools but in our culture at large. Our national drive to compete and achieve seems to be counter to kindness. As for myself, I have always felt that kindness has a synergistic effect. Kindness begets kindness. Kindness begets much more than kindness alone. When kindness is actively practiced in a classroom, learning is always enhanced and creativity flourishes. But why is this so?

Brain-based research has been investigating elements that support learning, documenting what exemplary teachers have always known through experience. By using PET scans to measure brain activity generated when a subject is involved in learning situations, the image allows us to envision the learning process as portions of the brain are highlighted. Through this process, researchers have been able to determine those conditions that enhance the learning experience. So what have we learned?

Stressful situations are counterproductive to learning. When the environment is supportive, respectful, and nonthreatening, the brain works most effectively to take in and process new learning. Kindness is the key. Kindness and all it implies must become a cornerstone embedded within all curriculums.

Talk of kindness in the classroom can quickly sound like edubabble. The question that ultimately arises is: What will this look like in tangible and concrete terms when one enters a classroom?

When one walks into the classroom where kindness is a cornerstone, signs and posters around the room immediately alert all who enter of the expectations of that classroom. A warm and friendly atmosphere immediately becomes apparent. And of course, science fills the room.

The agenda is posted on the board along with the homework assignments. There is a task waiting for the students. The tone is relaxed yet purposeful. It is evident that thought and preparation have been given to the lesson, as materials for the activity are laid out and ready to go, handouts prepared in advance. Such preparedness cannot be overemphasized in any classroom, but it takes on even more significance in a classroom that strives for a culture of kindness. Lack of planning and organization can put undue stress in a classroom situation, and that stress can be detrimental to the focus of kindness.

In addition, without organization and planning, the momentum of the lesson is broken, and students find themselves with idle time. Behavior problems, fooling around, or bullying can increase with undirected time. At the beginning of class, one will notice the teacher talking with a student or two as the day begins. Each day, there will be students who need some brief yet important individual time. The teacher recognizes them, listens, quickly addresses the individual concerns of the students, and moves on.

The teacher moves to the front of the room to begin today's lesson. "What is the significance of mitosis?" she asks. Several hands go up, and she calls on one boy who responds that, "It is cell division." With this answer, there are two possible choices the teacher could make. Kindness in the classroom is all about making choices. Biology teachers will recognize that this answer is not completely correct, yet it's not completely wrong, either.

The teacher responds: "That's true; cell division is very closely linked to mitosis, because when a cell divides, it must first replicate and equally separate the chromosomal material. Therefore mitosis, or division of the nucleus, is necessary for cell division."

The teacher recognizes that the student has taken a risk by raising his hand. Her response to this question will determine whether the student continues to stay involved in the rest of the lesson as well as how many other students volunteer in the future. Although the student's response didn't exactly match the question that was asked, the teacher uses it as a jumping stone, compliments the child for an answer, and then proceeds to draw out those elements of the response that she wants.

We need to keep in mind that the main point of questioning is to draw out the information being presented in the lesson while getting students to think on their own. If an answer to a question is viewed as wrong, the response goes nowhere. If the teacher receives even a wrong answer in an open manner, then the possibilities are limitless. With this in mind, we can also extend the approach to questions asked within the context of a lesson. The old saying that there is no such thing as a stupid question rings true when one considers kindness in the classroom. All questions should be received in this light.

Whether it is a question or an answer, students learn best in science classes where they feel free to take risks. Each time they take a risk, students are thinking and, therefore, should be validated.

The teacher uses a variety of instructional modalities to support a heterogeneous class. She writes words and definitions on the board while repeating them orally and uses diagrams on the board, pictures, or overheads to accommodate all learning styles. Kindness in the classroom is about respecting learning styles.

As the lesson proceeds into the day's activity or lab experience, the direction of the lesson changes and becomes student centered. Very often, the teacher forms students into cooperative learning groups or labs. Here, the pairing off or grouping of students becomes paramount and should be a deliberate consideration of the teacher. She must take into account learning styles, personalities, and interaction patterns as she groups her students so as to optimize constructive learning. The role of the teacher must change to facilitator; the real instruction is generated from within the peer groups.

She circulates to direct and assist students and is always conscious of the tone of the students' interactions. Are the students supportive and respectful of one another? Kindness is about consideration for one's peers. The learning comes from this consideration and respect for one's peers. Here in these small group learning situations, students must feel comfortable to take the risks necessary to construct learning. As they are free to take risks, they also feel validated by their peers.

I wish it were as simple as writing lesson plans that teach kindness, but it is not. We must model kindness and expect it of all students until the behavior becomes a habit in the classroom and part of the classroom culture. As I mentioned earlier, it seems to me that kindness is one of those things that is taught in kindergarten. However, unfortunately in today's world, this is not the case. Our students come to us with a great variety of entry levels with regard to this basic skill we'll call kindness. We cannot assume that kindness has been taught, expected, or practiced in the homes of our students.

A science classroom that strives for a culture of kindness doesn't just happen; it is the result of deliberate decisions and conscious choices being made on the part of the teacher. It is a classroom where everyone is welcomed and accepted. It is a classroom where one feels comfortable and able to take the necessary risks that enhance the constructive learning of science. It promotes the respect of learner to learner, learner to teacher, and teacher to learner. It embraces diversity of learning styles and creativity and enhances self-esteem.

THINKING: SUSAN H. DANA, MATH TEACHER, SCHOOL ADMINISTRATOR, ATHLETIC COACH

Susan H. Dana is the director of development at Kingswood-Oxford School in West Hartford, Connecticut, where she also coaches the girls' varsity lacrosse team. She is a graduate of Kingswood-Oxford School and was recently inducted into the school's inaugural Athletic Hall of Fame. Before returning to Kingswood-Oxford, she was the director of admissions and financial aid at Friends' Central School in Philadelphia, Pennsylvania, and varsity lacrosse coach there for fifteen years. In her final year there, her team won the Friends' League Championship for the first time in more than twenty years.

Sue received her BA in physical education from the University of Vermont (UVM) and her MA in educational administration from Temple University. After graduating from UVM, she played lacrosse at a national level for fifteen years, representing both New England and Philadelphia in national tournaments. During this same period, she taught math to middle school students at Kingswood-Oxford for six years and to high school students at

Friends' Central School for fourteen years. She was selected to the United States Trials Team, but due to an injury, she was unable to compete for the team.

She has coached field hockey, basketball, tennis, and lacrosse for more than twenty-five years. What follows is Sue's approach to teaching thinking skills through athletic coaching.

Sue Dana on Teaching Thinking

We have all heard the phrase "dumb jock." Indeed, growing up as a "tomboy" and, later, athlete, I have felt compelled to justify my intellect to both myself and others to counter that stereotype. I pursued athletics my entire life while always quickly explaining to friends and colleagues that I also love math and science, minoring in math in college and reading quantum physics books for fun. I do love math and science, but I wish I didn't have to explain that athletics and thinking can actually go hand in hand.

My nickname, given to me by my parents growing up, was "Scooter" because I could not stay still. I ran, played, climbed, jumped, and delighted in the physical. As I grew older, I gravitated to all sports and found that they just came naturally. I remember my first 440-yard race at the age of eight. I started out with the pack, held back through the first two turns, waited until the time "felt right," accelerated through the third turn, eyed the leader, picked up speed, and easily won, having passed five other runners. At the time, I didn't think I was thinking; I was just running.

In high school, I played on three varsity sports teams, field hockey, basketball, and softball, captaining all three and winning the award for the school's Most Outstanding Athlete as a senior. I also skied, played tennis, rode bikes, swam, and skated for recreation. In college, I played Division I basketball and decided to take up the sport of lacrosse, a sport my brother excelled at in high school. I ultimately captained the lacrosse team for three years. After college, I competed in lacrosse at a national level for fifteen years.

I never thought I ever had to think about sports. They just came naturally to me.

Growing up, at the genesis of Title IX, I yearned for a good coach but never had one until I was in my 30s. Perhaps that is why coaching was a natural for me. And it was only when I began coaching that I began to understand the connection between athletics and thinking.

Most would agree that good athletes have strong skills. But true athletes must be able to think, analyze, access, and problem solve. They must be able to see connections, weigh options, and determine the best strategies. Imagine if Michael Jordan, with all his innate athletic skill, lacked the ability to be innovative, flexible, and think creatively. He would merely be an average basketball player who could shoot, dribble, run, and jump.

When I teach ground ball pickups in lacrosse, I explain that the bottom hand must actually touch the ground to scoop and cradle the ball into the stick. I talk about the physics of levers and the need to cradle the ball fast to keep it in the stick. After years of coaching, I have learned that when I explain this skill from a mathematical and physics perspective, the players "get it." Creating an association to something that has a broader theoretical base helps the players to understand the skill and integrate it into their play.

I also believe that when we offer an atmosphere where students can question, reflect, and experiment, we create athletes who can access options, think for themselves, think critically and creatively, and construct solutions. For example, a player was reflecting on a game where we lost by two goals. I asked what she thought we could have done better. She responded, "We weren't picking up the ground balls and protecting our stick. All we were worried about was shooting on goal." It was clear, as we processed the action, that she realized that shooting on goal was not the zenith of the game. It was more about maintaining possession so that we could have more opportunities to both shoot on goal and keep the opponent from possessing the ball.

At least once a season, I devote an entire practice to a scrimmage where the players choose their own teams, call time-outs, run their own subbing, and coach themselves at halftime and the end of the game. I merely referee. I am always struck by the leadership that develops in the athletes, their analysis of situations and players, the solutions that emerge, and the way they learn to cooperate and support one another. This activity requires them to think about themselves and their teammates and collaborate with one another, all lessons they will need to be good citizens in the world.

Again, in lacrosse, I begin each season teaching the basic skills. It begins at the middle school level with how to hold the stick. There are any number of ways one can do this, but only one way allows for the strongest and most accurate catch and throw. To throw, one must reach back so the stick is parallel to the ground and facing 180 degrees from the target. The follow-through must be in an arc with the left hand ending up under the right armpit. Without a geometric understanding and description, a player will make mistakes and become easily frustrated.

I want the players to discover the connectedness of things. And when I teach a play, I always develop my practices around a particular skill. If it's an offensive play in lacrosse, I will often begin by putting out seven cones around the goal, one for each player. Before I give them a ball to use, I tell them that only one player may be at a cone at any time. They must discover for themselves that they need to keep moving, cut through and replace one another, shift, and create and use the space. Only when they have mastered this do we incorporate the ball. If it's a play that involves one or more picks (a method used to free a player from her defender), we begin the next few practices with that one pick as our opening drill. I want the players to notice and learn the connections between the individual skills and the free-flowing beauty of the team sport in motion.

Now, don't get me wrong. I believe that a strong coach sets high expectations, demands athletes to push themselves, sets the tone for each practice and game, teaches discipline, and demands respect. But I also believe that I can learn from my athletes. During a halftime talk, after I have given them three (and only three) concrete changes and/or suggestions, I always open up the discussion and allow the players to share their own observations. Sometimes they are right on, and other times they are misguided (and I tell them when that's the case). But the discussion allows them to be a part of the strategies, to listen to one another, to think about cause and effect, to compare and contrast, to see flaws, to understand another's arguments, to see connections, and to prepare their own. At the end of the game, we always meet, and they are, again, given the opportunity to ask clarifying questions, explain their thinking, and solve problems together.

Recently at the end of a game, a player of mine revealed to me that she finally understood the importance of ground ball control and pickups. She said, "Winning two ground balls is equivalent to scoring one goal." She was absolutely correct. She understood that the key to scoring was mastering the small details.

Players I have coached will tell you that my overriding philosophy is to "make your teammate look better." The assist is just as important as the goal, the goalie save begins the transition to the next goal, and the give-and-go down the field will create options for the rest of the team. Although we are out there to win, and few are as competitive as I am, I know that twenty years later, my players will never remember if they won or lost a particular game. But they will know that they were able to develop problem solving, collaboration, and analytical skills that will help them to be contributing members of their community. I recently had an alumna return to play in an alumni sports game. She said that in her job as an emergency room nurse, she has used the lessons she learned from lacrosse. She knows when to get help from others, she makes a point to acknowledge the work that others do, and she never tries to solve a crisis on her own just to make herself look good.

Now, I know that during all my years of playing and competing, I was not just randomly executing skills; I was developing cognitive and thinking skills that have been critical to my success in life. As an administrator, I have learned when to take a calculated risk and determine whether the risk is worth taking. I have learned how to access my strengths and challenges when asked to execute a particular plan. And as a coach, I hope imparting those cognitive skills to my players has helped them to be civic leaders in a democratic society. As leaders, they know that they play a critical part in creating an atmosphere where people want to participate. They have felt what it means to be part of a team, experiencing both the joy of winning as well as the responsibility that comes with each loss.

PROBLEM SOLVING:
GARY BLOMGREN, HIGH SCHOOL ART

Gary Blomgren earned his BS and MS in art education from Illinois State University. He holds an honorary MA from Marlboro College in Vermont for excellence in education. His teaching career spans 32 years and includes experience in K–12 and at the college level. At this time, he is the head of the Fine and Practical Arts Department and a teacher at Brattleboro Union High School in Vermont.

His forty-year career as a visual artist includes numerous shows and exhibits. At this time, his primary media include drawing, painting, and printmaking.

He is married, the father of four, and the grandfather of two. What follows are his thoughts on teaching problem solving through art.

Gary Blomgren on Teaching Problem Solving

Problem solving is an embedded part of a multifaceted process essential to the production of art. The solution is the work of art itself, while the problem has many possible origins, from the representation of a student's thoughts, dreams, or ideas to a question posed by the instructor. The pathway to the solution varies with each problem and may include parts or all of the discipline-based approaches in art education (studio production, art appreciation, aesthetics, and criticism) as well as standards established by national, state, or local education and art education organizations. In teaching, one hopes that students will continually re-examine the problem, process, and pathway, staying open to the possibility that the pathway may fork or turn to the right or left. Problems and their solving are rarely linear and never static (unless in a limiting artificial world). Rather, they are fluid and dynamic. Maintaining openness to the variety of possibilities is of paramount importance to a student's successful creative problem solving.

The teacher expects students to build up an understanding and ability to successfully communicate their ideas visually. To this end, students need to explore (through exercises) materials, techniques, design/composition as well as the work of other artists past and present. Exercises prepare the student with greater ability and understanding to create a final work of art. Table 6.1 presents one approach or pathway to creating a work of art.

Table 6.1.   An Artist's Creative Process

Intent	*Organization*	*Application*	*Completion*
Beginning with an artist's idea, thought, dream, or story and proceeding to . . .	. . . a visual plan applying design elements and principles . . .	. . . using media and techniques creating thumbnail sketches, progressing from rough drawing to a refined, finished . . .	. . . work of art.

On the surface, the process shown in Table 6.1 makes a complex journey seem simplistic. But it is far from it. Not stated in each area of the diagram, but demanded, is a great deal of questioning and, as such, problem solving. "What do I wish to communicate in my work?" "What colors, lines, and textures will best evoke the feeling I wish to produce?" "Does this large dark area lead the eye to the main area of importance in the picture?" "Should this shade of red be more intense?" "Does my artwork clearly communicate my intent?" I will apply these questions and many more to the lesson plan below.

Once the student achieves basic understanding, it is time to apply this knowledge in a final project. The solution to this visual problem (project) is always wrapped in a student's understanding of composition (essential to the success of all works of art), media (materials and techniques used to produce the work), and communication (the artist's intent).

For young artists to successfully determine their intent, they must conduct an investigation of feelings, ideas, and hopes about the world around them. In this way, the problem solving is genuine. The results are meaningful and serve a greater importance, which is their work of art. As students work through visual problem solving, they are constantly making decisions, from the simplest choice to the most complex solution. It is in this process that the instructor helps students work through questioning and gain greater abilities to think critically.

> **SAMPLE LESSON PLAN:**
> **"CHOICE MENU" PROJECT**
>
> The process of making connections and transforming the commonplace into new and unusual structures is a basic approach to building creativity. The assigned parts of this project will form a framework for you to complete your first major project in Advanced Studio Art. This project is a variation on a theme used regularly to get students back in the swing of drawing, communi-

cating, and creating successful compositions. In completing this work, the artist has unlimited variety of subject matter to combine and great latitude in the use of media.

Four subject matter categories must form the basic composition. Here are some possibilities.

Choice One: Architecture, Alphabet, Artist, Animal

Architecture: Select an element of architecture to include in your work. Elements could include doors, windows, stairways, post and lintel, archways, columns, etc.

Alphabet: Choose a font, a style of lettering, and include your initials. Size is at the discretion of the artist. These styles can be traditional or one of the many new fonts found on computers.

Artist: Give praise to your favorite by including an element from one of that artist's works. Use the work as a background or complete part or all of your composition in the chosen artist's style (this is called a pastiche).

Animal: Be it your animal spirit guide or totem, Fluffy your cat, an animal in a favorite story, or your Chinese fortune calendar animal (oh boy, can that be an experience), that animal should play a role in your composition.

Choice Two: Person, Place, Thing, Quote

Personal Image: This could be a self-portrait or some other image that symbolizes who you are.

Place: That special place that brings a joy and comfort to your soul or sole

Thing: An object of importance; a juju; something found, treasured, and kept—old or new.

Quotation: Words that speak to you, a saying, words of wisdom, fortune from a cookie, a song.

Choice Three: Border, Wall, Window, Beyond

Border: This is like a frame but perhaps uses a cyclical story line or new environment contrasting with what's to come in the center.

Wall: Imagine all the materials that a wall surface could be composed of—wood, stone, concrete, glass, paper, fur, or fabric. Is it an interior or exterior wall?

Window: The opening to another space or place, shaped perhaps like a gothic arch, or a traditional window with divided panes, a porthole, portal, door to . . .

Beyond: "Beyond" could be inside—out, deep space, shallow or a microscopic view, or an artist or fantasy world.

Four is the magic number in this assignment, and you need to select your own unique combination of four subject matters. The goal is to combine the four in a unified way that is meaningful to you, the artist, and to communicate that meaning successfully and visually.

Requirements

Art History: Find historical references for your work and be ready to present those during working and final critiques.

Reference Material: Have available visual references of the subject matter that you represent in your composition. These could be magazine pictures, photographs, photocopies from a library search, as well as pages from a variety of books located in the classroom.

Specifications

Media: All drawing media may be used as well as watercolor; we will reserve other paint media for future projects.

Support: Paper or board.

Size: 12" × 18" to 18" × 24".

Due Date: After instructor's introduction, one class day for referencing and thumbnail sketching, then ten working days to complete the final work of art. Expect one "work in progress" critique and a final critique.

Opportunities abound that demand students make decisions and, as such, solve problems. As the title of this assignment implies, each student must determine how to successfully combine a variety of subject matters into a unified whole. The whole must communicate something that is personally important and meaningful to him. Once the student determines the idea, she must answer an array of questions as to how all the parts will fit together to make a workable composition. This demands a student's attention to design elements and principles (composition).

Arguably, the number of elements and principles varies among teachers, but at least fourteen or fifteen exist. As we know, each of these design components has a myriad of subtle possibilities to consider. Students must also decide what to create with and on what surface, how big the work should be, and in what manner they will use the materials. During the production process, the student must periodically examine the work to decide its success and what, if any, changes he should make. The critique is an indispensable training tool of the instructor. It is through this experience that students often open to new possibilities, solidify their own thinking, and apply critical thinking to their work. The greatest decision may be the determination of when the work is done.

Creating works of art continues to have a magical, almost mystical quality. It's not to the level granted our distant ancestors, who produced their work in the deep reaches of caves and throughout the sacred places of their environment; still, a work of art results in a level of awe. One decision that each student must make is to believe that she can produce art. Art is not restricted to those born with that "special gift." Rather, it can be learned and developed by all.

The qualities essential to creative problem solving and the production of art are many, among them and not necessarily in this order are openness to the new, questioning, willingness to make mistakes—to take risks, suspension of judgment, positive/practical thinking, slowing down—taking time to "see" and think clearly, hard work and practice of concepts and techniques, concentration, observation, and patience.

COMMUNICATION: STEPHANIE ALDRICH, K/1 TEACHER

Stephanie Aldrich is a relatively new elementary teacher in a small K–8 school in Halifax, Vermont. Before this position, she taught preschool and early Head Start for three years. After receiving a BA from Marlboro College in Vermont, she was fortunate enough to complete her education degree at Antioch University New England in New Hampshire, a school that believes in nurturing the "hand, heart, and mind" of each child. According to Stephanie, "young children do not walk into school the blank slates that many people believe them to be. Every moment of their early lives has held a lesson in communication—milestones such as saying 'mama' and 'papa' and also more subtle lessons, such as knowing when to say please and when to pout to get your way. A teacher cannot and should not attempt to wipe clean this slate to rid children of some of their less preferable behaviors. What a teacher can do is provide the child with some more positive options." What follows is Stephanie's approach to teaching communication skills.

Stephanie Aldrich on Teaching Communication

Helping children to communicate effectively in a primary classroom involves multiple steps. First, one must establish a comfortable, nurturing environment where children feel safe enough to take risks in front of their teacher and peers. Next, the teacher builds the expectation that children will listen and respond to the thoughts of their classmates. Lastly, discussion topics and problems must have more than one approach or answer to give the children a reason to actively listen to one another.

In my current role as a K/1 teacher in a rural Vermont school, establishing a safe and risk-taking environment takes continual effort and patience. Some children are risk takers by nature, and my goal is to get them to channel this energy into appropriate academic outlets. My daredevil Chris, who will stand on one foot on the rocking chair, is not always so brave when he is trying to sound out and write a word. Young children quickly develop a notion that there is a right way and a wrong way to do assignments. When

I look at Chris's paper and celebrate his work—"Look! You knew that *b*, *l*, and *n* are all in balloon!"—I am telling him that it is okay to take chances. Instead of looking for what's missing, the focus should be on the knowledge the student is demonstrating.

Establishing the expectation that children will listen to their peers is a difficult process. Young children are inherently self-interested and often can relate to their classmates only if they have shared a similar experience. Sharing time gives classic examples of this. Little Kelly goes up in front of the class with a beautiful shell she found on vacation and tells all about it. When it comes time for questions and comments, the other children respond with things like "I went to the beach once with my family and it was really hot but I took my shoes off anyways and we ate ice cream." While this comment is somewhat related, it has moved the situation away from communication into parallel expression. Kelly's time to communicate with the class has been taken over by a new student. Many children have now moved on to thinking about hot days and ice cream. I feel it is important to shift the focus back onto the child who was sharing, modeling a way for the other children to build on their own experiences.

"You said that you spent a hot day at the beach and that you had ice cream. Maybe you could ask Kelly if it was hot when she went to the beach, or if they had treats to eat that day?" With repeat practice the students will learn to make connections between their thoughts and experiences and those of their peers. This is a basic building block of effective communication.

Once one has established the environment and expectations, one can introduce situations that lend themselves to communication. Math problem solving is one of my favorite areas for developing this skill. The reason for this is simple. Most people think that the point of math is to get the one right answer. In reality, math is about trying different approaches, making connections, and being able to explain your thinking.

Before I ask children to work individually on a problem, I will ask them to share a strategy that they might use to solve the problem. Children without a strategy will need to listen actively to their peers to find a way to approach the problem. Students with strategies can improve their work by listening to other approaches and thinking about which approach is most effective.

After the children have finished working on the problem, we will have a short time planned to share work on the board. I'll have two or three students go to the board at the same time and write out their work. They will then have a few minutes to explain their thinking.

Some of the most effective lessons in communication come from wrong answers. A teacher could simply tell a student, "That's not the answer—it's seven," and the student would most likely accept it. But if a teacher lets the students decide what the right answer is, wrong answers hold new value.

They become possibilities that can be argued and considered. Likewise, the student with the correct answer must defend and explain it. All students involved are learning to consider different points of view and to challenge their own assumptions. These are key skills in meaningful communication.

With my kindergartners, we only walk through the basics of this process, keeping work-share time brief. The first graders have more confidence in their ability and are readier to take risks. Next year, they will be ready for even more responsibility. Hopefully, this will lay the groundwork for the rest of their schooling. If they can move through the grades ready to take risks and share ideas, they will be developing skills that are invaluable in the adult world.

INTEGRATING THE FOUR FUNDAMENTALS

Kindness, thinking, problem solving, and communication can be a part of all subjects at all ages, as the reader can see from the four accounts above. One can also see the interdependence of these four fundamentals of curriculum. In each example, the teacher must include references to the more than one of the four foundations, even while concentrating on only one. Belle speaks of communication skills while she discusses kindness in her biology class. Gary cannot separate problem solving from thinking and communication in art. Sue's teaching thinking through athletic coaching necessarily includes problem solving, kindness, and community. Stephanie concentrates on communication with her K/1 students, but at the same time, she is teaching them to be kind to one another during discussion and to express their thinking with those communication skills. Our four foundations of curriculum are also the fundamentals of rich, productive, and cooperative living.

Conclusion

A period of intense writing teaches as much to the writer as the writer intends to tell his readers. Writing this book has been no different. I began by composing an article in response to a call for pieces on the theme of educating the whole child by a professional journal. My words survived the first cut but ultimately did not find a place in print.

The article then began to grow into the book you now hold in your hands. At the same time, I grew as well, both as educator and human being. What started as an angry response to some of the aspects of the No Child Left Behind Act (NCLBA) evolved into something bigger, something with more power. I can now see that NCLBA is not the problem. It is a symptom of larger issues. The law is an attempt, albeit political, to address the issues of education in the United States.

Interestingly, the evolution of the book shares some parallels with my own evolution as a teacher and as a person. When I begin a project, I usually have a good idea of where it is going, but the more deeply involved I become, the more the project takes on its own life, becoming an organic process. So it was here. So it is with most creative processes.

I have been an educator for thirty-two years. I have been alive for fifty-four. When I began my career as a teacher, I probably would have applauded the new standards and accountability movement because I believed in nothing but intellectual rigor. I was determined to climb the professional ladder, thin as it was, in education. I would be a hero by demanding that students give their best, write correctly, and appreciate the great works of literature. I would advance naturally to an administrative position from which I could spread my gospel of traditional, white male educational values.

My ideal vision defined the purpose of education as passing on the culture, preparing the next generation to take its rightful place as educated members of society. There was no room for such frivolity as late work, nonstandard English, or poor spelling. I branded students who acted out in my classroom as "problems"; often they were individuals with some kind of psychological issue to work through.

I would call parents to let them know that their sons and daughters merely had to try harder to succeed at the levels of which they were capable. After all, that was what I had done. Indeed, I progressed through the ranks quite quickly, taking courses, completing degrees, and initiating large projects and seeing them through.

I became a department head, a principal, a central office administrator. Along the way, though, my vision of the world began to change. Many times, I could not understand why others did not agree with me, why students did not simply do as they were told, why parents challenged me when I gave them less than great news about their children.

Colleagues would get angry with me, disagreeing with what I was trying to do. Politics, budgets, and school boards would all get in the way. About halfway into my career, I began to soften considerably. I realized that students were all different, people were afraid of change, the world was evolving, and those in power did not want anyone to rock their comfortable boats. I could see that many educational decisions were in fact not educational decisions at all but either financial or political decisions.

A bigger picture emerged, grander than reading and writing and math. The bigger picture included humane qualities such as understanding, kindness, empathy, caring, and community. Good writing changes the writer. So does good teaching, and so does good living. Writing this book, which began in anger, led me to a position of hope and courage. My anger will not accomplish much, but hard work, based on the desire to improve the spiritual as well as intellectual quality of people's lives, just might have an impact.

As an educator, I see that impact coming through the school, along with many other sectors of our community. However, school is the place I have staked my territory, and education is the arena of my efforts.

NCLBA is an attempt to improve America's schools. The law demands that schools be accountable for their work. There is nothing wrong with that. The law demands that we do more to close the learning gap between rich and poor, minority and majority, and disabled and able. There is nothing wrong with that. In fact, NCLBA is an embarrassment to the public education system, since it points out the many problems most of us have known to be there all along.

The elephant in the room has sneezed, and there is no turning back now. The problem, as I see it, is that NCLBA applies simplistic solutions to complex problems and looks at education generally through the wrong side of the telescope.

I have seen literally thousands of students over the years. Each one is unique, with gifts and flaws, an imperfect gem, human, needing love and attention. Now I see what I could not see before, blinded by my own vision of achievement. I did not see any problem with standardized tests, but I have come to realize that there are no standardized students. Sometimes I think that our nation confuses legal and biological equality. Yes, we are all equal before the law, but no, we are not all equal with respect to physical and mental characteristics. As Nell Noddings says, "Many youngsters have alternative, genuine talents, but these are disregarded" (Noddings 2007, 29). She further reminds us that "students do not come to us as standard raw material, and we should not expect to produce standard academic results" (32).

Setting a third-grade standard as a guideline is one thing, but demanding that every student meet that standard in third grade is entirely different. We cannot educate people as if they are all peas in one pod. My understanding is that a standards-driven educational system varies time, not the standard, while a traditional educational system keeps time fixed and varies the standards.

In other words, a regular system gives a student 180 days to pass Algebra I. Passing can be any grade of sixty or more out of one hundred. A standards-based system defines the standards to be met, and then students work toward them until achievement. One child may finish Algebra I in a month, while another might take two years. The point is that both students, once they have met the standards, know the same amount of math.

I believe that most educators and people in general would agree that students learn at different rates and in different ways. I once heard a joke related to this issue of standards: What do you call the person who finishes last in his class at medical school? The answer is "doctor." Every student who completes medical school masters the material to some preset standard. Unfortunately, I suspect that some who do not make it could if they were given more time or perhaps different teaching methods.

We now have as many as fifty sets of standards and many different measurement tools. Somehow, we have created a national curriculum without creating a national curriculum. In the process, the various national organizations devoted to each of the disciplines, such as the National Council of Teachers of Mathematics, have published their own standards as models.

Of course, having a group of people dedicated to that particular discipline writing the set of standards for that discipline has its own set of problems. The result is a massive atomization of the curriculum and trying to claim importance for everything. Vermont, the state in which I have worked for most of my career, currently has over 150 standards, and these are further broken up into sets of grade expectations, defining what students need to know and be able to do at the end of each grade level, K–12. The mind spins at the thought.

As my research progressed during the writing of this book, my thinking developed in response. I could not simply be angry at NCLBA without offering good reasons and at least an attempt at another way of doing business. That other way of doing business became the heart of the book. Let's first turn the telescope around and look at the big pieces, not lots of tiny little ones. What are the underlying, basic building blocks of an effective, powerful curriculum?

The other question I began to ask was about the purpose of education in general. Are we really concerned with nothing more than supplying the workforce with what it wants to remain economically competitive in the global marketplace? Does every person have to go to college to be successful? Are we in such desperate need for engineers? (I thought we couldn't get math teachers because they were all going into engineering to make more money.) Is there only one definition to the quality of life, and does that definition stop at economic success?

Throughout life, one meets many individuals who are happy but not wealthy. For example, religious orders of monks can lead very fulfilled lives without needing many if any possessions. In the secular world, some people own small farms, run corner groceries, or perhaps labor as salespeople. While not all of them are happy, certainly many are. There has to be more to life than preparing to go to work.

If the sole or primary purpose of schools in America is to prepare individuals for the workforce, then I fear we may be heading toward a *1984*-like vision of the world. Schools prepare students according to a prescribed set of standards, and then those students are "sold" to the highest bidder in the marketplace. Human beings are reduced to the level of a commodity.

I do not argue against preparing individuals to be self-sufficient, productive members of our society. This is a noble and practical purpose. However, I also argue that it is not enough.

Looking at the larger picture, I argue in this book that the ultimate purpose of education is to prepare individuals to act as fully involved members of a democratic society. This purpose subsumes workforce readiness, since participating in a democracy involves being a productive member of the society and community. Too many people, myself having often been one of them, are unhappy in their work. Having the specific skills for work is not enough; that would be to ignore the spiritual, creative aspect of human existence. To return to the beginnings of this book, the original article from which it grew, we have to consider the whole child.

William Wordsworth tells us that "Getting and spending, we lay waste our powers." (Perkins 1967, 289) Our power is our potential for creativity, joy, community, love of nature, spiritual advancement, and appreciation for life in all of its glory. These powers make us human. We must not lose sight of these characteristics in our rush to cram more and more information into our curricula to reach ever-higher levels of education leading to greater economic productivity, inevitably resulting in a consumer society. "Getting and spending," we may be losing our souls.

The Association for Supervision and Curriculum Development's Commission on the Whole Child released its report in 2007. An article in *Education Week* summarizes some of the report as suggesting that "the definition of a successful student has to change from one whose achievement is measured solely on the basis of test scores to one who is healthy, emotionally and physically inspired, engaged in the arts, and prepared for employment in a global economy" (Honawar 2007, 7). While this statement moves beyond the narrow test-centered culture of the moment, it still falls short of moving beyond job preparedness.

Preparing our students for life in a democracy is more about teaching them what to do and how to be than things to know. A democracy is a form of government in which the people make the decisions. For that to happen, they have to be able to get along with one another so as to listen carefully to the various sides of an issue, separate the good ideas from the less effective ones, and finally come to a consensus on what to do. If we do not teach basic kindness, which allows this type of conversation to take place, then (and we see it in our government already) we will become separated into groups of people who share the same tunnel vision.

How can we declare that some states are red and some blue, as if the entire state is Republican or Democratic? In any number of those states, the "red" or "blue" votes prevailed by less than 3 or 4 percent in the last presidential election. The collective wisdom of the people is destroyed if we succumb to such factional pressure. One way to avoid it is to teach that all people, all ideas, and all points of view have worth. They are worthy of being listened to, examined, debated, and ultimately incorporated or rejected from the final solution for specific and logical reasons.

San Diego school superintendent Carl A. Cohn sees the danger in a single, top-down model when he speaks of the dangers of criticizing NCLBA.

> These attacks [on the education system] allowed those in charge to portray themselves as the defenders of children, to justify any means to promote their model of improving student achievement, and to view their critics through the same apocalyptic lens of good and evil that has characterized many of our recent national debates. . . . On a national level, it has had a chilling effect on open discussion and prevented a genuine national debate on the goals of the No Child Left Behind legislation. (2007, 32)

How can any society exist without kindness? History is sadly replete with examples of one group of people destroying another in the name of ethnic cleansing as opposed to learning to live in peaceful coexistence. The process continues to the present day. Learning to live together in peace may very well be the single most important concept we can teach our children. If students of mine leave me with no other knowledge, skill, or habit but tolerance, I feel successful.

If individuals are to debate issues meaningfully, then they must learn to think. By charging the populace with the task of making decisions for the country, we are assuming that they can build, analyze, and defend an argument with intelligence and energy. Debates on the major issues that affect our lives cannot be reduced to sound bites, nor can they be based on emotions or faulty logic. Again, Noddings picks up this idea when she writes about the job of a teacher: "Another part is to encourage our students to think and take responsibility for their own expanded learning" (2007, 32).

A good example would be the No Child Left Behind Act itself. The law states that all children should reach the standards by the year 2014. To argue against this would be political suicide. How can someone say that not all students are going to make it—and that that is an acceptable position? However, simple logic dictates that a goal of 100 percent is not possible due to natural statistical fluctuations. At a meeting of the National School Boards Association Council of School Attorneys, "Washington lawyer John W. Borkowski likened the law's demands to a basketball tournament in which every team must win" (Walsh 2007, 18).

Are we then saying that by the year 2014, all public schools will be deemed failing schools? The year 2014 seems far away, so perhaps there is not so much pressure to look at that future date. In the meantime, believing that every child will be proficient in reading and writing on grade level is a wonderful idea. The problems here are obvious, however, including the lack of solid direction on how we are going to reach this impossible goal. San Diego superintendent of schools John Cohn sums up the situation neatly when he says, "Beginning with the legislation's title, federal lawmakers succeeded in codifying the good intentions and misconceptions of a generation of education reformers." He goes on to say, "I believe there is a place where no child is left behind, where all children achieve grade-level proficiency and there is no achievement gap. It is called heaven" (2007, 32).

In the short run, the law can create a good feeling, but in the end, it is a false promise and a false hope. Our preparation of students should include arming them against feel-good rhetoric as well as providing them with the knowledge of logic necessary to construct and deconstruct arguments. Then, if kindness prevails, civilized and informed debate can follow, leading to solid, practical, and productive decisions.

No one can doubt that our nation as well as our world faces enormous problems, from armed conflict to global warming to poverty. A crucial skill that our schools must teach is how to solve problems of all types. Kindness and thinking allow for civilized debate and the search for answers. The search for answers is problem solving. According to Noddings,

> Students must be asked to identify for themselves the important points in every unit of study, construct their own summaries, attempt problems that have no obvious solutions, engage in interpretation, and evaluate conflicting explanations and points of view. (2007, 32)

Returning to the preservation of democracy, we can see that the society in which we live must work toward solving the problems that plague it. The workforce is demanding individuals who can work together, think, and discover the answers to many issues. As we teach the steps toward problem solving, we should remember to make the process explicit in all subjects until students internalize this skill. Noddings points out that teachers can pose interesting and challenging problems in "cooking, chemistry, photography, mechanics, and everything else the schools offer" (2007, 29).

Once again, teachers must help students to recognize the value of metacognition and reflection. Stopping at the first solution may not be the best method. Reflecting on other possibilities and comparing those to the initial answer may very well lead to better and better results. Citizens need the ability to compare, critique, and defend various courses of action to make informed and helpful decisions. NCLBA certainly asks that we test students in math, but it does not say much about problem solving specifically, nor does it say anything about expanding the concept of problem solving as a method of meeting all of life head-on. In fact, the only subjects for which the law demands accountability are math and reading and, soon, science. We do not even test writing.

The cliché that what gets tested gets taught applies here. If schools face sanctions based on students' scores on tests of mathematics and reading, then these two subjects receive the lion's share of attention. Those human powers mentioned above are left to those who can afford them. Can it be fair to close the learning gap in reading and math at the expense of music, art, foreign language, and social studies? Do we allow these other courses for those who meet the math and reading standards only? Or for those who can afford to buy their way out of the public system?

In other words, we are simply redefining the achievement gap by allowing those students who traditionally do well in the current academic setting, generally those from the higher socioeconomic layers of our culture, to continue to pursue those other courses, while the less fortunate spend all of their time working to catch up on the tests. The irony is that courses such as music and art can have a profound effect on students' ability to learn in all areas. They also enrich the quality of life.

What NCLBA misses are the broad human skills. One of those, communication beyond reading, provides the fourth foundation block for a curriculum that supports democracy. All the other skills are near useless if we cannot communicate, sending and receiving information. A democratic society rests on communication among its people. We have to share information and understand information, not have it control us in the form of slippery rhetoric, emotional appeal, or propaganda.

The ability to communicate releases our spirits. Music, dance, art, song, poetry, acting, and creative writing all provide avenues for creative release. Even if we cannot produce all of these media, at the very least we should be able to understand and appreciate them. Different cultures communicate in various ways, so we must prepare students to withhold judgment. We must aim our educational efforts at teaching students to seek understanding before reacting. The ability to communicate is one of the primary characteristics that set us apart from other species on the planet.

One of the memorable points made in the U.S. Department of Education's 1983 *A Nation at Risk* was that, had another country forced our own education system on us, we would have seen it as an act of war. America has always risen to the occasion in a crisis. We are in crisis now, but there is a distinct difference between the current crisis in education and other crises, such as the Great Depression or the bombing of Pearl Harbor.

During the Depression, the pain of economic despair was everywhere. People had to help one another, deal with sacrifice and hardship, and face difficult challenges of basic need daily. That was when many of the elements of the current social agenda were begun, and the nation took care of itself as individuals came together to take care of each other.

When Japan attacked Pear Harbor, the United States entered World War II. There was rationing and materials shortages, and many human lives sacrificed. The country shared a common suffering, and we once again rose to the challenge, together, amassing an army and all the equipment necessary to ultimately overcome our enemies.

Now, however, the nature of our crisis is different. It is insidious. We are slowly drowning in a sea of "getting and spending." We have become numbed by the overwhelming amount and availability of consumer goods. Of course, there are still people in poverty, hunger, and homelessness. Yet, the general state of the country is comfort, and those at the top are not aware of any generalized suffering. Even the war in Iraq has not resulted in the nation as a whole giving up something for the war effort, such as gasoline or aluminum, as in World War II. To be sure, individual families have lost their loved ones, a horrible loss beyond words. Yet, the United States of America remains a world leader and a rich nation.

By focusing so hard on the economic mission of schools, we are turning away from the larger mission, which is to nurture whole human beings, including their spirits, for participation in what should be the greatest democracy in the world. We seem to have forgotten the greater good for economic and political supremacy. Any student who completed an education that had as one of its basic tenets "kindness" could not tolerate the divide between rich and poor, the presence of hungry children and homeless people, and the lack of medical care.

The comparison has been made many times, but I think it bears repeating here: think of how much we could do with the money spent on one week of the war in Iraq, or even with the funding for one major weapon. If our educational system taught kindness and communication in the way defined by this book, we might not need those weapons and wars. I would argue that we do not need to be the richest or most politically powerful nation in the world to remain a world leader. We do need to redefine *leadership* and *power*.

Perhaps our nation is at an evolutionary crossroads in its development as a culture and member of the world community. We are a nation at risk—at risk of losing its soul. It is not yet too late to rekindle the spirit of America. We can make decisions that will set the direction of history for decades to come, and we can enact those decisions through the schools by rearranging our priorities and definitions.

For instance, why are we so desperate for more engineers? Do we need yet smaller cell phones, faster computers, higher definition televisions? Why not reroute the efforts of science to the causes of developing nonfossil fuels, ending hunger, upgrading medical technology and availability, and providing everyone with decent housing? What are we doing? Where are our humane values? What has happened to the free, open, and informed debate of democracy?

We could lead the world in a new direction: one of peace, prosperity, and health. By creating a new world-class curriculum based on kindness, thinking, problem solving, and communication, the United States could exhibit the courage necessary to lead the world in a better direction. This is not a watering down of the educational system. In fact, I see it as just the opposite. What I am calling for is a revolution in education that would catapult us into a new age.

Starting with the four pillars of curriculum, we would build our educational system by asking how each topic of instruction can be connected to kindness, thinking, problem solving, and communication. We would lose no academic rigor, but we would gain a new perspective on what schools are all about and a new set of emphases or purposes to guide our work. The primary purpose of education would shift from preparation for the workforce to preparation for life in the fullest sense as well as preparation for active community and democratic involvement.

We would emphasize compassion in our world. We would teach tolerance. We would use our skills of thinking, problem solving, and communication to better the lot of all people, not just some. I apologize for the epiphanic and apocalyptic tone developing here, but I do believe that we are looking at a profound point of decision. Our educational system, by and large, is becoming the product of an increasingly diminished view of the human spirit and an old, stale view of leadership and economic quality of life. With education on the national table, we have an opportunity to do it right.

Clearly, I have set out an overwhelming task, but the stakes are high and thus warrant such expansive thinking and planning. What is at risk here is nothing less than our future and our humanity. The Depression was overwhelming. World War II was overwhelming. In this nation's finest moments, we have met the overwhelming and overcome it. We can do this again if we are willing to muster the political will, drive, and selflessness required.

I am calling for nothing less than a general reconceptualizing of our educational system, its goals, and its methods. We will have to put aside our differences to come together to create a solution that addresses the needs of many. Even more difficult will be redefining the meanings of "global leadership" and "quality of life."

As I have mentioned before, the United States may be the richest nation on earth, but it does not rank first in quality of life according to United Nations reports. Despite our wealth, there is much poverty in our nation along with hunger, homelessness, crime, and political unrest. We do not even have the lowest infant mortality rate. To me, this is appalling. We need to adjust our values as a country, and the best way to accomplish this is through our one most universal institution, the public schools.

While NCLBA is an attempt to bring about some of the change I am suggesting, it is a meager effort. Despite its enormous length and numerous demands, it primarily insists that students reach basic levels of proficiency in two or three areas: reading, mathematics, and science. If this law has caused so much controversy, I can only imagine the obstacles to moving in the direction I am suggesting.

Nevertheless, this is not a reason to give up. I have often referred to myself as a cynical idealist. Thirty-two years in education have given me much to be cynical about, but I keep trying anyway. Our children and our future are too important to let them slip away into a world of raw commercialism. We need to stop the train now, while there is any chance remaining.

I am not very politically astute, nor do I have experience with change on a grand scale, so I readily admit that I do not have a solid plan for implementing my ideas. I must leave that to others far more talented than I. What I can offer, though, is a broad outline of possible steps we might take toward achieving the goals set forth in this book. We must begin with redefining the quality of life and restoring the values of our democracy.

No one whom I know is permanently happy. However, one needs a few basic elements to lead a relatively happy, quality life. A person has to have enough to eat, a comfortable place to live, meaningful work, self-worth, positive relationships with others and the earth, and spiritual enrichment. There is no necessity for excessive wealth, extravagant or overabundant amounts of food, or overly spacious homes. Having, perhaps, a little more than we need is the key.

Rather than atomizing the curriculum, we begin with the four foundations: kindness, thinking, problem solving, and communication. We build our overarching objectives based on these four elements, with preparing students for life in a democratic society as the defining purpose of education. We will ultimately need to have thousands of small meetings within communities, each leading to meetings in larger and larger communities, to define overarching objectives. The system will not be designed by educators alone, nor by communities alone, nor by politicians alone. An educational system must reflect the core values of a society, even if only a few can represent consensus.

Some overarching objectives I might suggest would include the following:

1. Tolerance
2. Compassion
3. Logical thinking skills
4. Collaborative working skills
5. Public speaking, writing, self-expression skills
6. Responsibility
7. Reflection
8. Consensus-building skills
9. Community awareness
10. Working knowledge of math and science
11. Care for the earth
12. Skills necessary for meaningful and profitable employment
13. Spiritual fulfillment
14. Participation in the arts

These fourteen goals, or whatever list of overarching objectives the nation defines, would then drive curriculum in the same way that standards are supposed to. Each goal fits one or more of the basic blocks, taking it a bit further. The next step would be to build courses of study, or sequences of learning activities, based on these foundations and goals. The general process is one of beginning with the big picture, then refining that into actual learning activities.

I am presenting an oversimplification here, since the actual process would necessarily be much more detailed. The point is that we should start from the point of view of quality of life in a democracy as opposed to the skills necessary to build a workforce that will support the position of richest nation in the global economy.

Do we want a nation of riches and anxiety or a nation of comfort and ease? Do we want a nation of cogs in a workforce machine or a nation of individuals who perform work that gives them satisfaction and meaning? Do we want a nation of haves and have-nots, or do we want a nation where certainly some excel economically while others struggle, but for the most part, the vast majority enjoy lives of comfort? Do we want to live as rich people, or do we want to live as people with rich lives?

This new system would necessarily have some fundamental differences in teaching strategy and student assessment compared to what we have now. We would see teachers working in teams and students working on individual and team projects. I do not think that one can learn the kinds of broad concepts we are working with here without integrating instruction through solving real-world problems in real-world settings. The school would become a busy place of students coming and going as they study matters of interest to them.

There would also have to be courses that look much as they do now. There will always be fundamental skills that students must master to engage real-world problems meaningfully. Sometimes, the nature of the problem will dictate which skills a student needs to learn at a particular time. The flexibility here is something we have seen before, though never on such a grand scale. However, if it is all bound together through kindness, thinking, problem solving, and communication, a web will define the common agenda and maintain focus for everyone.

The manner of assessment can no longer be single high-stakes tests in this system. We want students to show their learning through demonstrations of mastering concepts in context. In other words, the students investigate and solve problems in a real context and then demonstrate or present their work to panels of judges composed of teachers, community members, and experts in the field of the presentation. Schools such as Dennis Littky's the Met Center in Providence, Rhode Island, do this now.

Joseph DiMartino, president of the Center for Secondary School Redesign, discusses this issue of assessment.

> The dominant school improvement strategy of standards-based accountability stresses academic content and standardized tests. Performance assessment combines content with skills, and requires students to carry out tasks to demonstrate mastery of both. The tasks generally fall into three categories—performance, portfolios, and projects—and are designed to encourage students to think and to solve problems through hands-on activities. (2007, 44)

He goes on to say that

> because performance assessments focus on tasks linked to curricula and state standards, they drive testing in a positive way; the tasks are worth teaching to,

because their mastery indicates that students have learned both the material and how to use it. (2007, 44)

The schools and curriculum I am recommending both reflect and build a society that values quality of life over economic supremacy. Spiritual well-being replaces mere workplace readiness and potential earning and buying power. Leadership is about taking the world in a healthier direction than we are currently going. Truly, we are talking about an evolutionary step for the human race.

We can do this. NCLB is the first step, putting so many vital issues on the national political table. Now we must rethink those issues in a more thorough and radical manner. America must rebuild its schools from the ground up, not from the top down. We must rebuild our schools as humane institutions, which teach the skills and values that equip students to live the good life, one enriched by spiritual values, compassion, meaningful employment, comfort, and democratic involvement.

There is still time, and we can do this. America can be the leader of a new age.

Appendix

This appendix is designed to assist teachers in embedding kindness, thinking, problem solving, and communications in their lessons. For each of these curricular foundations, there are three graphic organizers. One is a general template, suggesting some factors a teacher might want to consider regarding the particular foundation piece under consideration. The second template is completed for an actual lesson. The third template is blank, so the teacher can use it for actual planning purposes.

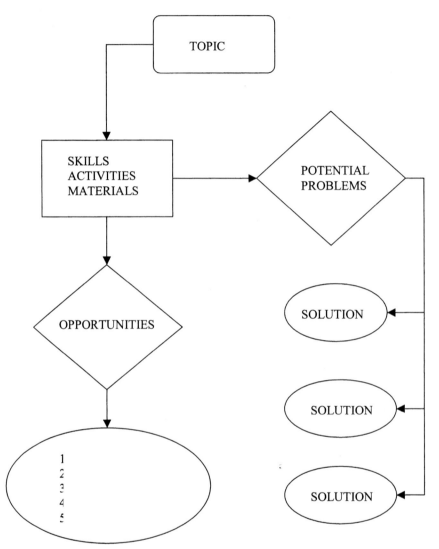

Figure A.1.   Planning Sheet for Maximizing Kindness during a Lesson

Given the lesson or unit you plan to teach, where might opportunities and problems in kindness likely occur? Can you anticipate them? How will you capitalize on the opportunities? Can you strategize solutions to use before or as the problems occur?

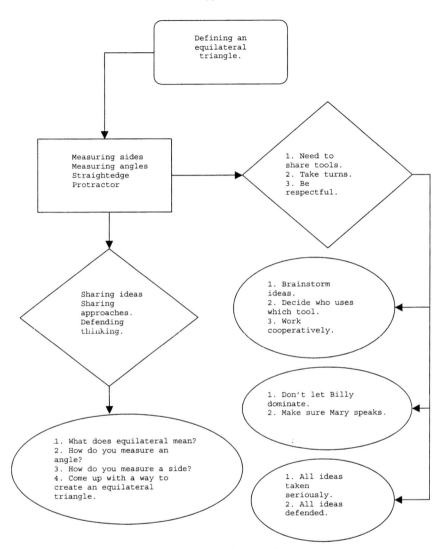

Figure A.2.   Planning Sheet for Maximizing Kindness during a Lesson

Given the lesson or unit you plan to teach, where might opportunities and problems in kindness likely occur? Can you anticipate them? How will you capitalize on the opportunities? Can you strategize solutions to use before or as the problems occur?

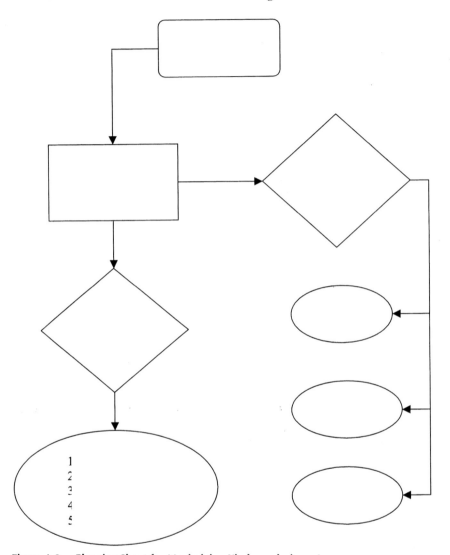

Figure A.3. Planning Sheet for Maximizing Kindness during a Lesson

Given the lesson or unit you plan to teach, where might opportunities and problems in kindness likely occur? Can you anticipate them? How will you capitalize on the opportunities? Can you strategize solutions to use before or as the problems occur?

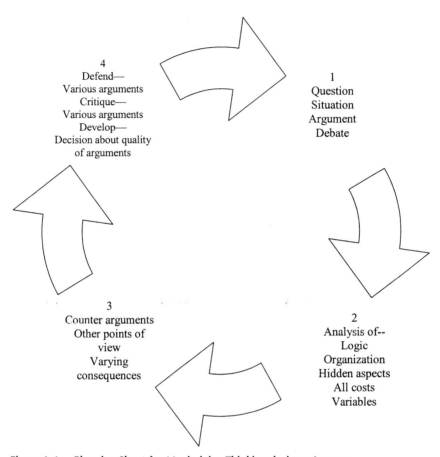

Figure A.4.   Planning Sheet for Maximizing Thinking during a Lesson

Given the lesson or unit you plan to teach, where might opportunities and problems in kindness likely occur? Can you anticipate them? How will you capitalize on the opportunities? Can you strategize solutions to use before or as the problems occur?

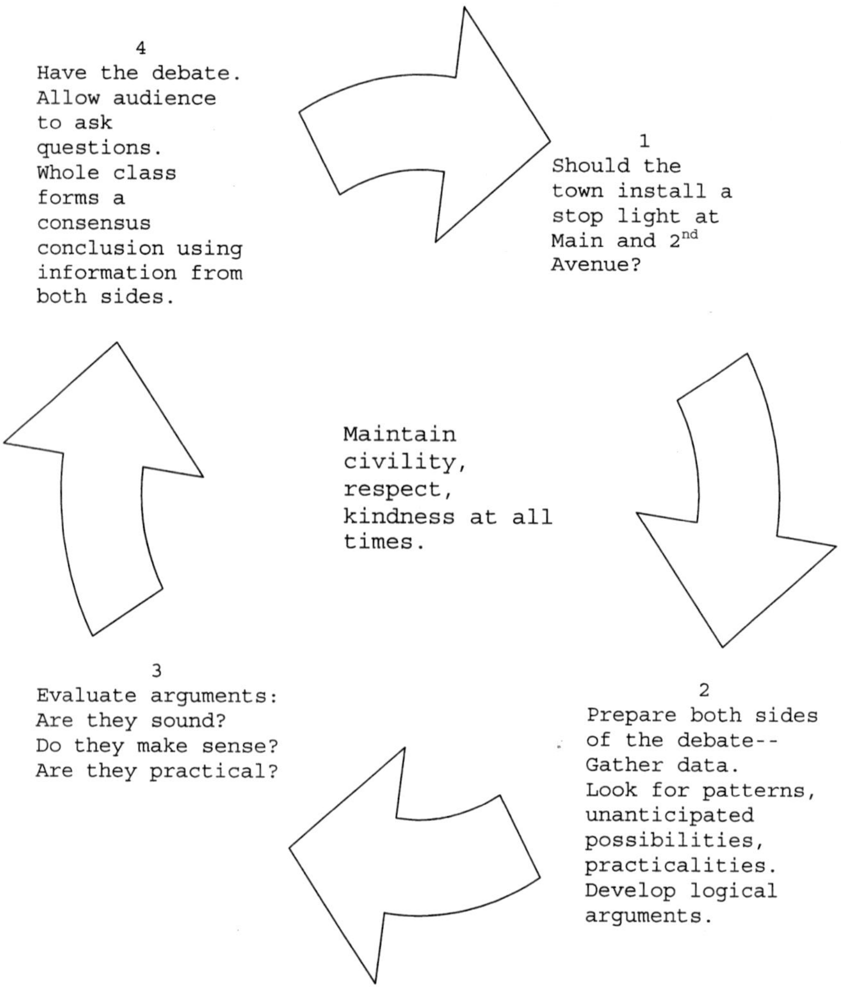

4
Have the debate.
Allow audience
to ask
questions.
Whole class
forms a
consensus
conclusion using
information from
both sides.

1
Should the
town install a
stop light at
Main and 2nd
Avenue?

Maintain
civility,
respect,
kindness at all
times.

3
Evaluate arguments:
Are they sound?
Do they make sense?
Are they practical?

2
Prepare both sides
of the debate--
Gather data.
Look for patterns,
unanticipated
possibilities,
practicalities.
Develop logical
arguments.

Figure A.5.   Planning Sheet for Maximizing Thinking during a Lesson

Given the lesson or unit you plan to teach, where might opportunities and problems in kindness likely occur? Can you anticipate them? How will you capitalize on the opportunities? Can you strategize solutions to use before or as the problems occur?

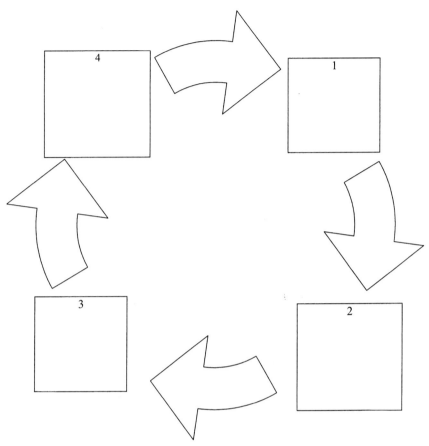

Figure A.6.   Planning Sheet for Maximizing Thinking during a Lesson

Given the lesson or unit you plan to teach, where might opportunities and problems in kindness likely occur? Can you anticipate them? How will you capitalize on the opportunities? Can you strategize solutions to use before or as the problems occur?

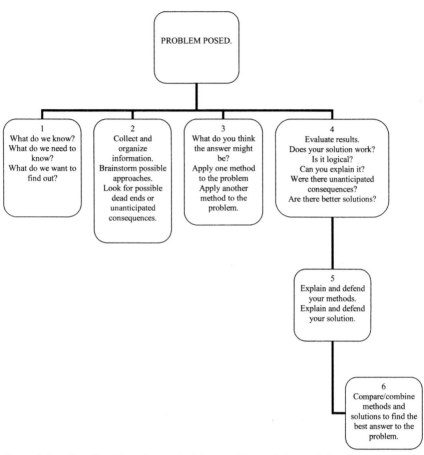

Figure A.7.   Planning Sheet for Maximizing Problem-Solving Activity during a Lesson

Given the lesson or unit you plan to teach, where might opportunities and problems in kindness likely occur? Can you anticipate them? How will you capitalize on the opportunities? Can you strategize solutions to use before or as the problems occur?

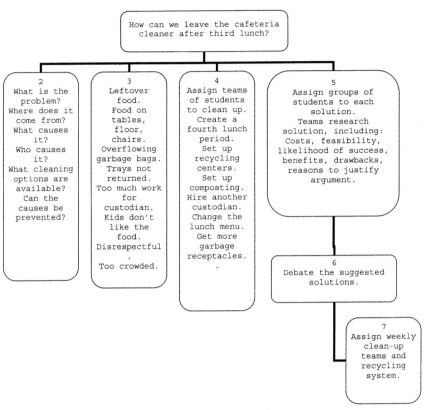

Figure A.8. Planning Sheet for Maximizing Problem-Solving Activity during a Lesson

Given the lesson or unit you plan to teach, where might opportunities and problems in kindness likely occur? Can you anticipate them? How will you capitalize on the opportunities? Can you strategize solutions to use before or as the problems occur?

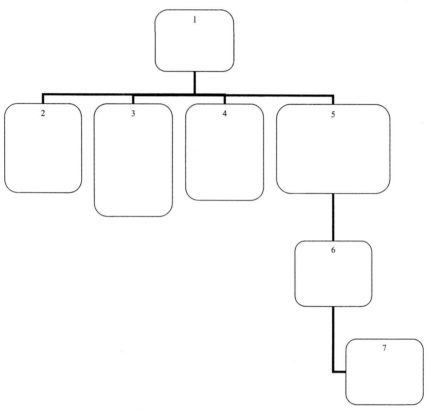

Figure A.9.   Planning Sheet for Maximizing Problem-Solving Activity during a Lesson

Given the lesson or unit you plan to teach, where might opportunities and problems in kindness likely occur? Can you anticipate them? How will you capitalize on the opportunities? Can you strategize solutions to use before or as the problems occur?

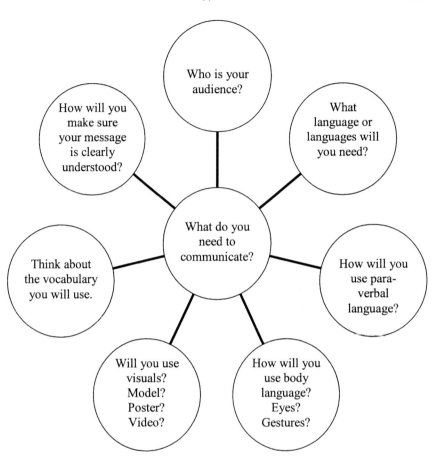

Figure A.10. Planning Sheet for Maximizing Communication Activity during a Lesson

Given the lesson or unit you plan to teach, where might opportunities and problems in kindness likely occur? Can you anticipate them? How will you capitalize on the opportunities? Can you strategize solutions to use before or as the problems occur?

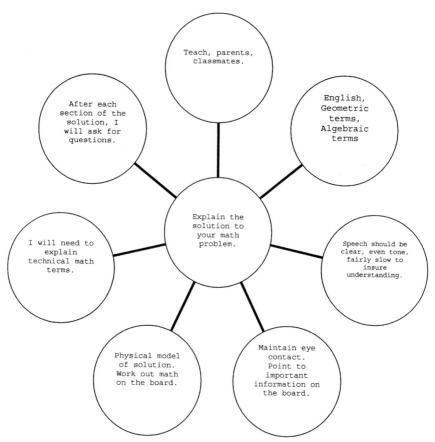

Figure A.11.   Planning Sheet for Maximizing Communication Activity during a Lesson

Given the lesson or unit you plan to teach, where might opportunities and problems in kindness likely occur? Can you anticipate them? How will you capitalize on the opportunities? Can you strategize solutions to use before or as the problems occur?

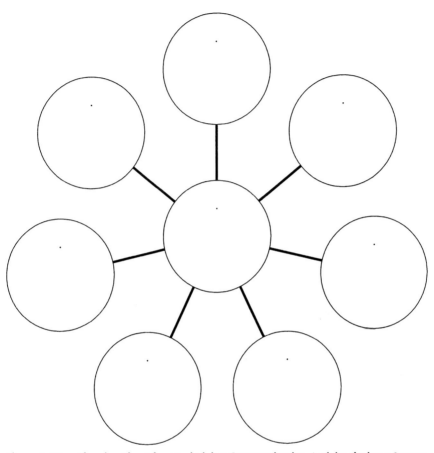

Figure A.12.   Planning Sheet for Maximizing Communication Activity during a Lesson

Given the lesson or unit you plan to teach, where might opportunities and problems in kindness likely occur? Can you anticipate them? How will you capitalize on the opportunities? Can you strategize solutions to use before or as the problems occur?

References

Allegrante, J. P. 2004. Unfit to learn. *Education Week* 24 (December 1): 38.

Allen, R. 2003. The democratic aims of service learning. *Educational Leadership* 60 (March): 51–54.

ASCD Community. 2005. *Education Update* 47 (October): 5, 7.

Bahrampour, T. 2005. Arlington parents wonder: Why add Italian class? *Washington Post.* January 1. www.washingtonpost.com/ac2/wp-dyn/A49936-2005Jan30? (accessed February 19, 2005).

Bailey, et al. 2006. *Mathematics: Applications and concepts, Teacher's Edition.* New York: McGraw Hill/Glencoe.

Beach, R. 1993. *Reader-response theories.* Urbana, Ill.: National Council of Teachers of English.

Berglund, N. 2004. Norway still the world's best place to live. *Aftenposten* (Norway). July 15. www.aftenposten.no/english/local/article828724.ece (accessed April 22, 2007).

Berliner, D. and S. Nichols. 2007. High-stakes testing is putting the nation at risk. *Education Week* 26 (March 14): 48, 36.

Borja, R. 2005. Business leaders call for more cooperation in K–12 giving efforts. *Education Week* 25 (September 28): 6.

———. 2007a. Project launches 10-year initiative to link early education, economy. *Education Week* 26 (March 14): 12.

———. 2007b. Scholars push ideas to bolster U.S. workforce. *Education Week* 26 (February 21): 7.

Boyer, P. 2005. What would Ernie Boyer say? *Education Week* 25 (August 31): 40–41.

Bracey, G. W. 2005. Education's "groundhog day." *Education Week* 24 (February 2): 38–39.

Bradley, A. 2004. Arts educator wins prestigious award. *Education Week* 24 (December 8): 4.

Brooks, J. and M. Brooks. 1999. *The Case for the Constructivist Classroom.* Alexandria, Va.: Association of Supervision and Curriculum Development.

Carter, R. 1998. *Mapping the mind.* Berkeley, Calif.: University of California Press.

Cavanagh, S. 2005. Concept of "work readiness" credential gains supporters. *Education Week* 24 (February 23): 19.

———. 2006. Big cities credit conceptual math for higher scores. *Education Week* 25 (January 11): 1, 14.

———. 2007. Colo. rejects more math, science requisites. *Education Week* 26 (April 4): 19, 21.

Checkley, K. 2005. Resiliency and achievement. *Education Update* 47 (October 2005): 6, 8.

Cohn, C. A. 2007. Empowering those at the bottom beats punishing them from the top. *Education Week* 26 (April 25): 31–32.

Consortium of National Arts Education Associations. 1994. *National standards for arts education.* Reston, Va.: Music Educators National Conference.

Cooper, J. E. 2002. Constructivist leadership: Its evolving narrative. In *The constructivist leader,* 2nd ed., L. Lambert et al., 112–126. New York: Teachers College Press.

Covey, S. R. 1989. *The seven habits of highly effective people.* New York: Fireside.

Dewey, J. 1938. *Experience and education.* New York: Kappa Delta Pi/CollierBooks.

DiMartino, J. 2007. Accountability, or mastery. *Education Week* 26 (April 25): 44.

Education Week. 2007a. Public school's role. *Education Week* 26 (February 21): 13.

———. 2007b. Service learning. *Education Week* 26 (April 11): 14.

Eisner, E. 2003. Preparing for today and tomorrow. *Educational Leadership* 61 (December/January): 6–10.

———. 2005. Back to whole. *Educational Leadership* 63 (September): 14–18.

Epstein, R. 2007. Let's abolish high school. *Education Week* 26 (April 4): 40, 28.

Finders, M. J. 1997. *Just girls: Hidden literacies and life in junior high.* Urbana, Ill.: National Council of Teachers of English.

Fitzhugh, W. 2004. Romantic fiction. *Education Week* 24 (September 15): 35.

Foote, C., P. Vermette, and C. Battaglia. 2001. *Constructivist strategies.* Larchmont, N.Y.: Eye On Education.

Foster, H. M. 1979. *The new literacy: The language of film and television.* Urbana, Ill.: National Council of Teachers of English.

Frank, M. 2002. *Math yellow pages.* Nashville, Tenn.: Incentive Publications, Inc.

Gardner, H. and J. Walters. 1993. A rounded version. In *Multiple intelligences: The theory in practice,* H. Gardner, 13–34. New York: Basic Books.

Gewertz, C. 2005. Training focuses on teachers' expectations. *Education Week* 24 (April 6): 1, 14.

———. 2006. H.S. dropouts say lack of motivation top reason to quit. *Education Week* 25 (March 8): 1, 14.

Given, B. 2002. *Teaching to the brain's natural learning systems.* Alexandria, Va.: Association for Supervision and Curriculum Development.

Goleman, D. 1995. *Emotional intelligence.* New York: Bantam Books.

Hammond, B. G. 2005. On dropping AP courses. *Education Week* 24 (January 19): 32.

Hirsch, E. D. 1987. *Cultural Literacy: What every American needs to know.* Boston: Houghton Mifflin Company.

Hoff, D. J. 2006. Big business going to bat for NCLB. *Education Week* 26 (October 18): 1, 24.

Honawar, V. 2005. U.S. leaders fret over students' math and science weaknesses. *Education Week* 25 (September 14): 1, 13.

———. 2007. Curriculum-development group urges focus shift to whole child. *Education Week* 26 (March 28): 7.

Hyerle, D. 1995. *Thinking maps: Tools for learning.* Cary, N.C.: Thinking Maps, Inc.

Jacobson, L. 2005a. Book spells out "core curriculum" for teacher training. *Education Week* 24 (March 2): 10.

———. 2005b. Study: Quality of 1st grade teachers plays key role. *Education Week* 25 (September 21): 3, 16.

———. 2006. Studies connect behavior, reading. *Education Week* 25 (February 22): 8.

Jensen, E. 1998. *Teaching with the brain in mind.* Alexandria, Va.: Association for Supervision and Curriculum Development.

Johnson, G., R. Poliner, and S. Bonaiuto. 2005. Learning throughout the day. *Educational Leadership* 63 (September): 59–63.

Kamil, M. L. and H. J. Walberg. (2005, Jamuryzc). The scientific teaching of reading. *Education Week* 24 (20), 38, 40.

Kennedy, X. J. 1990. *An introduction to poetry.* New York: HarperCollins.

Klein, B., J. D. McNeil, and L. A. Stout. 2005. The achievement gap. *Education Week* 25 (November 16): 32.

Kober, N. 2007. *Why we still need public schools: Public education for the common good.* Washington, D.C.: Center on Education Policy.

Kohn, A. 2004. Feel-bad education. *Education Week* 24 (September 15): 44, 36.

Lambert, L., D. Walker, D. P. Zimmerman, J. E. Cooper, M. D. Lambert, M. E. Gardner, and M. Szabo. 2002. *The constructivist leader.* New York: Teachers College Press.

Lerner, B. 2005. Why teach biography? *Education Week* 24 (March 16): 37.

Littky, D. and S. Grabelle. 2004. *The big picture.* Alexandria, Va.: Association for Supervision and Curriculum Development.

Manzo, K. K. 2004. Writing skills. *Education Week* 24 (September 29): 11.

———. 2005. States make gains in international studies. *Education Week* 25 (December 14): 13.

———. 2006. Graduates can't master college text. *Education Week* 25 (March 1): 1, 16.

———. 2007. Teachers say testing deters use of current events. *Education Week* 26 (January 24): 12.

Marzano, R. 2003. *What works in schools.* Alexandria, Va.: Association for Supervision and Curriculum Development.

McLaughlin, M. and M. Blank. 2004. Creating a culture of attachment. *Education Week* 24 (November 10): 34–35.

Miller, J. J. 2007. Can political participation be taught? *Education Week* 26 (February 21): 36.

Morrill, R. 2007. Monopoly and "No Child Left Behind." *Education Week* 26 (April 11): 34.

Moses, M., D. Livingston, and E. Asp. 2005. If college is the answer, what are the questions? *Education Week* 24 (June 22): 45, 47.

National Council of Teachers of English and International Reading Association. 1996. *Standards for the English language arts.* Urbana, Ill., and Newark, Del.: National Council of Teachers of English & International Reading Association.

National Council of Teachers of Mathematics. 2000. *Principles and standards for school mathematics: An overview.* Reston, Va.: National Council of Teachers of Mathematics.

National Research Council. 1995. *National science education standards.* Washington, D.C.: National Academy Press.

Noddings, N. 2005a. *The challenge to care in schools,* 2nd ed. New York: Teachers College Press.

———. 2005b. What does it mean to educate the whole child? *Educational Leadership* 63 (September): 8–13.

———. 2007. The new anti-intellectualism in America. *Education Week* 26 (March 21): 29, 32.

O'Brien, T. C. 2007. Mathematics and the pure in heart. *Education Week* 26 (February 28): 30–31.

Olson, K. 2006. The wounds of schooling. *Education Week* 26 (November 8): 28–29.

Olson, L. 2006. As states feel pressed to revisit standards, calls are being renewed to tighten them. *Education Week* 26 (October 18): 1, 15.

Paige, R. and M. Huckabee. 2005. Putting arts education front and center. *Education Week* 24 (January 26): 52, 40.

Palmer, P. J. 1998. *The courage to teach.* San Francisco: Jossey-Bass.

Perkins, D., ed. 1967. *English Romantic Writers.* Harcourt, Brace & World, Inc. N. Y.

Porter, J. 1997. Lecture on nonverbal behaviors delivered June 10, Mt. Kisco, N.Y. Brookfield, WI: National Crisis Prevention Institute, Inc.

Resnick, A. M. 2007. Educatocracy. *Education Week* 26 (March 7): 26–27.

Richard, A. 2004. Governors urge high school reforms as a top priority. *Education Week* 24 (November 24): 8.

Roberts, T. 2004. The discipline of wonder. *Education Week* 24 (September 29): 31.

Rose, M. 2005. How should we think about intelligence? *Education Week* 24 (September 22): 40–41.

Rosenblatt, L. M. 1965. *Literature as exploration.* New York: The Modern Language Association of America.

Samuels, C. A. 2007. Panel weighs NCLB and students with disabilities. *Education Week* 26 (April 4): 22.

Sapphier, J. and R. Gower. 1997. *The skillful teacher.* Carlisle, Mass.: Research for Better Teaching.

Senge, P. M. 1990. *The fifth discipline.* New York: Doubleday.

Short, K., J. Schroeder, J. Laird, G. Kauffman, M. Ferguson, and K. Crawford. 1996. *Learning together through inquiry: From Columbus to integrated curriculum.* Portland, Maine: Stenhouse.

Sternberg, R. J. 2004. A dozen reasons why the No Child Left Behind Act is failing our schools. *Education Week* 24 (October 27): 65, 42.

Stigler, J. W. and J. Hiebert. 1999. *The Teaching Gap.* New York: The Free Press.

Stotsky, S. 2004. How to read Shakespeare or bus schedules. *Education Week* 24 (December 8): 30.

Stronge, J. H. 2002. *Qualities of effective teachers.* Alexandria, Va.: Association for Supervision and Curriculum Development.

Sylwester, R. 1995. *A celebration of neurons.* Alexandria, Va.: Association for Supervision and Curriculum Development.

Trojcak, D. 1971. Developing a competency for sequencing instruction. In *Developing teacher competencies,* ed. J. E. Wiegand, 131–165. Englewood Cliffs, N.J.: Prentice-Hall.

Vermont Department of Education. 2000. *Vermont's framework of standards and learning opportunities.* Montpelier, Vt.: Vermont Department of Education.

Vermont Department of Education and Vermont Institute for Science, Math and Technology. 1997. *Vermont elementary and middle level mathematics portfolio scoring guide.* Montpelier, Vt.: Vermont Department of Education.

Viadero, D. 2004. Declaration calls for more caring environments in schools. *Education Week* 24 (September 8): 10.

Wagner, T. 2006. Rigor on trial. *Education Week* 25 (January 11): 28–29.

Walsh, M. 2007. Clinton criticizes testing required by NCLB. *Education Week* 26 (April 25): 5, 18.

Zimmerman, D. P. 2002. The linguistics of leadership. In *The Constructivist Leader,* L. Lambert et al., 89–111. New York: Teachers College Press.

About the Author

Daniel A. Heller has been an educator since 1975. He holds both an BA and MA in English from Middlebury College in Vermont, an MEd in curriculum and instruction from Keene (New Hampshire) State College, and a certificate of advanced graduate studies in educational administration and planning from the University of Vermont. Besides teaching, Dan has served as a department head, director of professional development, principal, and district curriculum coordinator. He has presented on educational topics throughout the United States and in Canada and China. He has published one other book, *Teachers Wanted: Attracting and Retaining Good Teachers* (2004), along with numerous articles, chapters, and columns for the Association for Supervision and Curriculum Development, Phi Delta Kappa, the National Council of Teachers of English, and others. He has spent most of his career in Vermont, where he lives with his wife of thirty-two years, Nina. He can be reached at helrdan@yahoo.com.